THE NINE LIVES
OF POPULATION CONTROL

MICHAEL CROMARTIE is a senior fellow and director of the Evangelical Studies Project at the Ethics and Public Policy Center in Washington, D.C. He is the co-editor, with Richard John Neuhaus, of *Piety and Politics: Evangelicals and Fundamentalists Confront the World,* and the editor of *Disciples and Democracy: Religious Conservatives and the Future of American Politics, Might and Right After the Cold War,* and other volumes.

The Nine Lives
of Population Control

Edited by

MICHAEL CROMARTIE

Midge Decter ▪ Nicholas Eberstadt ▪ Gilbert Meilaender
Amartya Sen ▪ Julian Simon ▪ George Weigel
Karl Zinsmeister ▪ *and others*

ETHICS AND PUBLIC POLICY CENTER
WASHINGTON, D.C.

WILLIAM B. EERDMANS PUBLISHING COMPANY
GRAND RAPIDS, MICHIGAN

136325

Copyright © 1995 by the Ethics and Public Policy Center
1015 Fifteenth St. N.W., Washington, D.C. 20005

Published jointly 1995 by the Ethics and Public Policy Center and
Wm. B. Eerdmans Publishing Co.
255 Jefferson Ave. S.E., Grand Rapids, Mich. 49503

Printed in the United States of America

00 99 98 97 96 95   7 6 5 4 3 2 1

Library of Congress Cataloging-in-Publication Data

The nine lives of population control / edited by Michael Cromartie . . . [et al].
p.   cm.
Includes bibliographical references (p.   ) and index.
ISBN 0-8028-0879-4 (pbk.: alk. paper)
1. Birth control. 2. Population policy. I. Cromartie, Michael.
II. Ethics and Public Policy Center (Washington, D.C.)
HQ766.N58   1995
304.6'66 — dc20   95-17413
CIP

Contents

Preface

Does our world now have more people than it can reasonably sustain? If current growth rates continue, will overpopulation be the cause of ever-increasing hunger, poverty, and environmental degradation? Will we run out of resources? And if the world is becoming overpopulated, what is the most wise, humane, and effective response by concerned governments and non-governmental organizations?

Conversely, is "overpopulation" a fiction that threatens to distort public policy and, more gravely, do enormous damage to the dignity of human lives?

These were some of the issues that engaged twenty-six scholars and practitioners at a conference sponsored by the Ethics and Public Policy Center in October 1993. For a day and a half, the participants engaged in a lively and stimulating exchange centered on four papers, under the theme "Is There a World Population Problem? A Challenge to the Conventional Wisdom."

Eleven months later, issues of this kind were laid out on a much larger table at a huge U.N.-sponsored gathering in Cairo. The third International Conference on Population and Development was foreseen by many as a golden opportunity to establish a new category of human rights: "reproductive rights," with the right to abortion-on-demand at its heart. But this agenda met with a surprising amount of resistance, as we shall see in chapter five.

The four papers and two related responses from the Center's 1993 conference form the nucleus of this book. Social critic and writer

Midge Decter examines the philosophical and ideological underpinnings of anti-natalist positions and concludes that the issue of "control" lies at the heart of the population controversy. She traces the course of the population-control movement from the birth of "eugenics" in 1883, through the efforts of Margaret Sanger and Planned Parenthood, on to the present and the influence of the radical feminists and ecologists.

Nicholas Eberstadt, of Harvard University and the American Enterprise Institute, looks at the modern idea that a government should have a population "policy" by which it attempts to shape the size, composition, and rate of change of the national population. It is a serious misconception, he says, to assume that scientific "population studies" have established a clear causal relationship between population change and economic or social change. In responding to Eberstadt, **Robert Engelman** of Population Action International asserts that population activists mostly see themselves as working to increase rather than diminish human freedom, especially among poorer women. He argues that there are legitimate grounds for supporting some new interventions because risks to health and development seem to accompany rapid population growth in some countries.

In a collaborative effort, the well-known economist and population theorist **Julian Simon** joins **Karl Zinsmeister**, editor of *The American Enterprise,* to examine how alarmist visions of population growth continue to form the conventional wisdom, despite compelling evidence to the contrary. They point out that the success of a country's development depends largely on its political and economic system and not on the size of its population. The implication that people are social, ecological, and economic nuisances is dangerous, they say. World Bank economist **Rodolfo Bulatao**, responding to Simon and Zinsmeister, deplores government coercion but defends voluntary population programs and focuses on the "huge unmet need" for family-planning services in the Third World. Both the Eberstadt and Simon/Zinsmeister sections are followed by edited excerpts from the lively ensuing discussion, under the heading "Comments."

Theologian and ethicist **Gilbert Meilaender** explores the meaning of parenthood, particularly within the perspective of Christian faith. Having children is "a venture in self-giving" that affirms "the fundamental goodness of life," he says. He suggests that while human reason and freedom may have a role to play in the "planning" of children, the desire to procreate springs from a deeper source of faith and hope.

Two other essays in this volume were not a part of the original conference. Harvard professor **Amartya Sen** provides a calm and clear overview of the population controversy, giving each side its due. "There is no imminent emergency that calls for a breathless response," he says. "What is called for is systematic support for people's own decisions to reduce family size through expanding education and health care, and through economic and social development." Sen's essay originally appeared in the *New York Review of Books*.

George Weigel, president of the Ethics and Public Policy Center, assesses the ideas that were debated before and during the remarkable Cairo Conference, which he says may have set in motion "moral and cultural dynamics that will, over time, result in the defeat of the radicals' agenda." Weigel documents the role that religious bodies (especially the Vatican) played in protesting the language and agenda of the Cairo draft document and argues that the planners of the conference "did not take account of the moral power of Pope John Paul II."

I would like to thank Carol Griffith for her superb editorial work and sage advice. A veteran writer at *Time* magazine told me years ago that she was the best editor in Washington, and I have discovered that he was not being hyperbolic. Eric Owens rendered diligent assistance, always with good cheer and high competence. Center interns Marcia Hurlbert and Jason Boffetti provided invaluable help, especially in transcribing the conference dialogue.

The Ethics and Public Policy Center's statement of purpose says in part that the Center strives "to deepen and broaden public debate on the ordering of our society and its relationship to the rest of the world," and "to foster a wiser moral and political debate across ideological barricades." We hope that, in wrestling with conflicting views of population, resources, economic and social development, and human freedom, this book will fulfill that purpose. We commend it to the attention of economists and demographers, political and religious leaders, environmentalists, and other concerned citizens.

MICHAEL CROMARTIE

The Nine Lives of Population Control

Midge Decter

The idea of population control, perhaps even the idea of population as we know it, seems to have come into circulation somewhere around the beginning of the nineteenth century. The Western world was in what is called "demographic transition," i.e., the ratio of people being born to those dying was growing larger each year. Actual numbers for the period are somewhat speculative, but it is said that between 1650 and 1850 the world's population more than doubled. The key element, according to Paul and Anna Ehrlich (in *The Population Explosion*),[1] was a marked decline in the death rate: at the beginning of the period, in agrarian societies without modern sanitation and medicine, an annual death rate of thirty-eight or more per thousand was characteristic, while by the nineteenth century, in certain European countries and North America, the death rate had gone down to thirty per thousand and below. The reason for this decline is clear. The Industrial Revolution, wherever its sway extended, was providing more and more people with better housing and nutrition and, even more importantly, was making possible new and effective systems of public sanitation.

Curiously, however, there is no record, either in the literature or in the social comment of the period, of any celebration of this devel-

Midge Decter is a distinguished fellow of the Institute on Religion and Public Life, in New York.

opment. No doubt the relatively sudden shift to a predominantly urban existence had created a widespread sense of social dislocation. In Britain and Western Europe, for example, simple crowding must have become palpable for people whose population had doubled in two hundred years and was well on its way toward doubling again. In 1798 Thomas Malthus had famously put it about that while population was increasing exponentially, the earth's food supply could at best be increased only arithmetically; thus, should war and pestilence fail to limit population and thereby forestall universal famine, "moral restraint," as he put it, would have to be applied. Moreover, especially in England, where the Industrial Revolution was born, many people must have begun to shudder along with William Blake at the sight of their villages and towns giving way before the spread of all those "dark, satanic mills."

The Birth of Eugenics

But something else was also dampening any possible stray gratitude for the benefits of better health and longer life. Industrialism was proving to be frighteningly promiscuous in its bestowal of benefits: just as mere millers and brewers and manufacturers were overtaking the landed gentry in wealth and power, the increase in the number of the poor made possible by improved rates of survival was lending ever greater significance—political as well as social—to their presence in society. So significant had this presence become that by 1883 Francis Galton, a cousin of Charles Darwin, had grown gravely concerned about the genetic stock of the nation. In that year he published his *Inquiries Into Human Faculty and Its Development,* and a movement to promote the science Galton named "eugenics" was born.

The eminent economist Peter Bauer, whose area of special concern has for many years been the economics of development, has noted a demographic phenomenon that might seem anomalous. For reasons that Bauer himself does not attempt to explain, in developing countries the accession of wealth leads individual families and sometimes whole clans to limit family size. We can only imagine why this happens: prosperity must give people, particularly those who have known poverty, a very different attitude toward both the present and the future than is normally found among the very poor—some sense of power over their destiny and over the possibilities open to their progeny. In any case, by the early nineteenth century, first in France and somewhat later elsewhere, fertility control of one kind or another came to be practiced by the middle class on a scale large enough to have at least some influence on the trend and distribution of the birth rate. (Not surprisingly, the United States, with an empty continent to settle, would for a time be an exception to this tendency among the industrializing nations.)

As the wealthy grew fewer in proportion, Galton was concerned about the growing demographic imbalance. He was worried by the consequences for future generations of the fact that the prosperous classes were so rapidly being outnumbered by the great unwashed. (We may hope that he was not including within the circle of his concern England's landed Tory aristocracy, who with few exceptions had remained just about as contentedly ignorant—not to mention unmannerly—as possible. It is valuable to remember that while the "masses" in England were reading, or being read to from, the Bible and *Pilgrim's Progress,* a goodly proportion of the "quality folk" spent their otherwise empty days riding to hounds.)

By 1923 Galton's worries had spread across the Atlantic. In that year the American Eugenics Society was founded, and overnight its cause became a highly fashionable one. The American birth rate was —in keeping with Peter Bauer's notion, predictably—going down, and at the same time immigration was being cut off; the question for the Americans had now shifted to one of how to "improve" the population that remained. Soon courses in eugenics were being taught in a number of colleges and universities, and the issue was being taken up by people across the political spectrum. The young Norman Thomas, for example, displaying a certain sense of social propriety that his socialism would never totally enable him to overcome, spoke with passion of "the alarming high birth rate of definitely inferior stock."[2]

By the 1930s, however, any idea of encouraging the better people to produce more children while "encouraging" the less desirables to produce many fewer—or, ideally, none at all—hit an enormous stumbling block: the Great Depression. Recently affluent people now suffering a sudden decline in prospects could hardly be urged to expand their families for the common good. Meanwhile, the second aspect of the eugenics project, i.e., controlling the birth rate of the undesirables, while legislatively highly successful (between 1907 and 1937, thirty-two states adopted legislation regulating the practice of sterilization for eugenic purposes), seems to have come up against certain difficulties of its own. For while the idea of forcibly sterilizing the undesirables may have been greeted with enthusiasm, the record of the actual practice bespeaks a certain reluctance on the part of the authorities appointed to carry it out. By the end of 1965, after more than half a century of practice, the total number of involuntary sterilizations was only around 65,000. From a different point of view, of course, 65,000 is not a negligible number. Still, the comparison with voluntary sterilization is instructive: beginning in the late 1950s, about 65,000 women were voluntarily undergoing tubal ligation, and about 45,000 men, vasectomy, each year.[3]

Margaret Sanger and Planned Parenthood

Meanwhile a radical, free-thinking woman named Margaret Sanger was traveling the world to find new and effective methods of contraception and to open birth-control clinics. Her passion was essentially a feminist one: to free women from the debilitation of excessive childbearing. (Her own mother, seriously ill with tuberculosis, had borne eleven children to a ne'er-do-well husband and had lived an exceedingly harsh life ending in an untimely death.) And as an early radical—as a friend and disciple of such figures as Big Bill Haywood, Emma Goldman, and, later, Havelock Ellis and H. G. Wells—she was also an impassioned advocate of sexual freedom, a freedom, as subsequent generations were to learn so well, made possible by the widespread distribution of effective contraceptives.

Mrs. Sanger was for a time an ally of the eugenicists, mainly because she and they had in common a bitter enemy: the Catholic Church. The alliance was, however, an uneasy one. Never known for being very concerned with the implications of her ideas, Sanger for a brief period supported coerced sterilization primarily as an act of defiance against the religious conservatives rather than on the strength of her own aspirations, which lay elsewhere. Surprisingly, in view of what became of her movement, she was no ardent fan of abortion, coerced or otherwise. Early on she did open a clinic in Brownsville, a Jewish slum in Brooklyn, that provided abortions (or what nowadays is called "abortion counseling"), but this was not what she really aspired to do, which was to prevent pregnancies in the first place. On their side, the eugenicists were uneasy as well. They feared for their respectability —which in the 1920s and even in the early 1930s was still considerable —should the world come to associate them with the effort to disseminate birth control, then still frowned upon in many circles.

In short, because Margaret Sanger could never quite overcome the anarchism of her early political education, her abiding instinct was to demand unlimited freedom, while that of the eugenicists was to impose control. (More than once in human history have the two inclinations found occasion to come together.) The irony was that the rise of Nazism was soon to give eugenics a black eye, whereas the birth-control movement was to go from strength to strength, mainly, it seems reasonable to suppose, because its declared aims were the health and freedom of women just as women were beginning to exercise a new degree of political power.

In the end, Sanger's success in forcing birth control out of the radical back alleys and into the mainstream of social action was to have unhappy consequences for her personally. By the early 1930s, she had managed to find more and more powerful support among men and women with names like Rockefeller, Duke, Scaife, Lasker, Sulzberger, and Dupont, and this very respectability would, finally, result in her own superannuation. Others in the movement began to think that following the leadership of a firebrand was no longer the proper strategy. In 1939 the various groups dedicated to promoting voluntary birth control were brought together under an umbrella called the Birth Control Federation of America—and men had begun to take over its leadership. Finally, three years later, to Sanger's great distress the organization changed its name to Planned Parenthood, thereby ostensibly placing greater emphasis on child spacing than on outright family limitation. The first director of the new organization was D. Kenneth Rose, chosen on the grounds that a man would have better access to the government bureaucracy.

The Population Council and the Pill

Another prominent player on the birth-control scene was John D. Rockefeller III, who had journeyed to Asia in the late 1940s and returned from there convinced that reducing the population in what came to be called the Third World took precedence over any Western efforts at economic development. Rockefeller called a conference of population scientists and put together a group called the Population Council. (An interesting sidelight is that he had wanted his own foundation to take on the project, but the foundation directors objected on the grounds that to do so would be offensive to the Church.)

Meanwhile, research into contraception was proceeding apace. Sanger, while not truly satisfied with it, had been pushing the combination of the diaphragm with spermicidal jelly, first devised by doctors in Holland. Then in 1956 Gregory Pincus and John Rock publicized their first findings about the Pill, and in the following year International Planned Parenthood and the Population Council were cooperating on a study of pill-takers in Los Angeles and Puerto Rico. The Pill was soon to become the contraceptive of choice of Planned Parenthood, at least for a time; but leaders of Rockefeller's Population Council, engaged as they were with the backward of the earth, were pessimistic about any techniques that required voluntary action on the part of poverty-stricken, downtrodden women. They were seeking to find some contraceptive method that would require little initiative and remain in effect for a long time. Subsequently they were to find it in the intrauterine device (IUD), which they and many members of the medical community distributed plentifully in the 1970s and 1980s—until it was shown that lodging a foreign object in the cervix carried a significant risk of pelvic infection. (The search goes on for passive contraception, the latest find, of course, being Norplant.) But in the end, like many other boons intended by the rich for the poor, birth control continued to find its most eager beneficiaries among the world's middle and upper-middle classes.

Although the impulse to control and reconstruct the population was never to die, Hitler for a time succeeded in making it a shameful impulse to own up to. But in the fullness of time it would find its way, curiously disguised, back into public discourse. Effective contraception may have helped to smooth the way, for, after all, birth control, even of the kind sought by Rockefeller, was clearly far more benign than the coercive medical practices associated with eugenics.

The Radical Feminists and the Ecologists

The year 1968 is a convenient point to begin, for in that year two separate anti-natalist movements—perhaps the most wildly anti-natalist in history—announced themselves to the world simultaneously: the radical feminists and the ecologists. Although their analyses as well as their aims were rather different, the combined force of their advocacies was enormous. The early radical feminists' most telling contribution was a loathing of sex, marriage, and motherhood that, having seeped quietly into the atmosphere through the offices of their more moderate (or maybe just less certain) successors, helped to condition American society to the idea of a woman's right to a government-funded abortion at any time during a pregnancy and for any reason.

This conditioning was important, not only in itself and as a catalyst for a more general moral erosion, but also for its suggestion of the ambition to godlikeness. The underlying assumption of the demand for total control of the creation of babies from beginning to end was that only masculine bad will or a malevolent social system stands in the way of reorganizing the very constitution of human life. Why should women continue to be, in Simone de Beauvoir's immortal words from her feminist classic *The Second Sex,* "subject to the species gnawing at their vitals"? Indeed, why should there not in the end be laboratories in which to breed babies and government institutions to bring them up as a newly just society wishes? As Shulamith Firestone put it in *The Dialectic of Sex* (1971): "Humanity can no longer afford to remain in the transitional stage between simple animal existence and full control of nature. And we are much closer to a major evolutionary jump, indeed to direction of our own evolution, than we are to a return to the animal kingdom from which we came."[4]

These radical feminists—the granddaughters, as it were, of Margaret Sanger, though prepared to go infinitely further than she—have cast a long shadow over the succeeding quarter-century, longer than many people realize. But in the end, having contributed more than a mite to the sum of human misery, they have left behind them few adherents. The ecologists, on the other hand, seem to have attracted disciples, both witting and unwitting, in every nook and cranny of the civilized world.

It is difficult to date movements, for they grow out of long-gestating ideas, but it was in 1968 that Garrett Hardin's famous article "The Tragedy of the Commons" appeared in the prestigious journal *Science*. What Hardin meant by "the commons" was the earth's natural resources, and he warned that, given the freedom granted by a society like ours to make use of these resources, we would soon be facing a natural catastrophe: "Ruin is the destination toward which all men rush, each pursuing his own best interest in a society that believes in the freedom of the commons. Freedom in a commons brings ruin to us all."[5]

For old Malthus, the non-renewable resource whose disappearance was so soon to bring world-wide famine had been farmland; for Garrett Hardin—though he would later prove to be more catholic in his worries—the main objects of concern in 1968 were soil, water, and, most particularly, fossil fuel. Malthus had not been able to foresee the prodigies of mechanized farming and new systems of irrigation and fertilization, or the possibility of creating whole new strains of grain, whose cultivation would be dubbed the Green Revolution. Hardin was naturally quite aware of all these developments, but for him and his confreres, such progress represented not a solution but the very heart of the problem. For if the early Industrial Revolution had doubled the population of the world in two hundred years, the explosion of economic advances in public health and medicine had more than doubled it again in half that time. Meanwhile, said the ecologists, we were simply using up the supply of all those resources that had made growth and health and prosperity possible. We were, it came to be said over and over, "eating our seed corn." Thus there were only two things to do: reduce population and reduce consumption.

All this is familiar by now, so familiar that we are in danger of losing sight of what was very new here in the story of eugenics and population control. Anxiety about the birth rate of the masses of still-agrarian Asia and Africa had for a long time been a popular cause, intensified by the spectacle of famine after famine attended by epidemic after epidemic. And though the American government had certain political difficulty in taking official part in any project to curtail population, such projects were being undertaken—to be sure, without notable success—through the combined forces of American private philanthropy and several agencies of the United Nations, such as the ILO, FAO, UNESCO, and WHO.

But for the ecology movement the problem was not located among the peoples of the agrarian Third World. It lay, rather, in the population of the industrialized West, and particularly with Americans. According to the ecologists, the American people had in the 1950s and 1960s grown rich beyond belief; and, enjoying, as they unfortunately did, the freedom to do whatever they wanted with their wealth, they had become a nation of little foxes spoiling the world's vines.

The Club of Rome, and ZPG

Not long after the publication of Hardin's article, a group of European industrialists calling themselves the Club of Rome produced a study—later discredited scientifically—claiming to demonstrate that American industry, by maintaining the American standard of living, was making the planet unlivable for everyone else. Each and every American baby being born would in his lifetime consume so much of the earth's precious and dwindling resources as to be an ecological disaster.

Now, the wish to find America responsible for the world's ills, as well as to rein in the country's economic system, nowhere in those years found a more sympathetic hearing than in the United States itself. We need not rehearse here why this was so, or the many and various forms in which this wish expressed itself. Suffice it to say that one of the major results of the campaign to "save the planet," reinforced by the new angry resistance to motherhood of some of America's best educated and most articulate young women, was a rebirth of the movement to exercise control over the country's population.

In time this movement would be expanded and enriched by the presence in our midst of the gravely disturbing population known in journalistic shorthand as "babies having babies." But to begin with, it was distinguished from its predecessors in that its main targets were not the poor but the rich. Zero Population Growth, the name given to the enterprise by Paul Ehrlich, one of its most visible and vocal advocates, addressed itself primarily to the qualities and habits of the advanced middle class. While the post-war baby boom was over, and births and deaths were now beginning to stay more or less in balance, the rate of resource depletion that resulted from the American standard of living, said ZPG, was already intolerable and would become more so unless a new sense of responsibility was fostered among the young. For, it was said, Americans were in the deathgrip of a false ideology, "growthism." Believing that economic growth promoted well-being, they were unable to recognize that growth is the disease, not the cure.

In case anyone might doubt that the United States, with its vast empty spaces, is overpopulated, Ehrlich instructs us that the impact of any human group on the environment has to be measured in terms of his formula, $I=PAT$: Impact equals Population times Affluence times Technology. Overpopulation, then, does not mean overcrowding as such but refers to the number of people in any given area relative to its resources. (In other words, no matter how deplorable the conditions in which they live, the poor of Africa make exemplary citizens of the earth, for they live on a continent immeasurably rich in resources and yet they avail themselves of very few of these.) Also, in Ehrlich's view, "the flow of immigration [into the United States] should be damped, simply because the world can't afford more Americans."[6] Several kinds of disasters are said to follow inevitably from the "population explosion": hunger, leading to epidemics; ozone-depleting gases and acid rain, leading to destruction of the ecosystems; and even, because of increased international competition over scarce resources, the ever greater likelihood of a nuclear holocaust.

While nuclear holocaust seems to have receded from the list of guaranteed woes, the other dire predictions continue to circulate through the country's consciousness, and continue as well to titillate all those, both at home and abroad, who share eagerly in the process of indicting America.[7] The result of the spread of the ecological mindset has been the imposition of a variety of regulations upon the country's public institutions and industries, as well as upon the private conduct of its citizens, never before contemplated.

Much has occurred in recent years to assuage the earliest anxieties of Zero Population Growth. Abortion has been not only nationally legalized but declared a constitutional right. Contraception has become ever more effective and widespread; school systems in the country's major cities are distributing condoms among schoolchildren (so far to no great effect), and bribing young black girls to use Norplant is now at least under discussion. A significant number of the baby boomers, coming of age in the 1960s, were induced through a heady combination of philosophy, ambition, and greed to put off having children until very late in the biological game, thus burdening the world with many fewer new consumers than they might have.

The Need for Control

What then is the problem? The problem, for Ehrlich and company, is twofold. First, family planning continues to focus on the needs of individuals and couples; what we need is population control, which will focus on the needs of society. Second, while "the basic biological and physical science of the human dilemma is well enough understood to permit sound recommendations for immediate action . . . almost no work has been done on ways to make the needed conversions in the economic systems so that scientific recommendations can be implemented with a minimum of disruption."[8] In other words, the problem is still freedom, that damnable freedom about which Garrett Hardin had earlier waxed eloquent. "So long as power and responsibility are separated," Hardin said, "population control is impossible."[9]

We know from historical as well as present experience that there is only one way in which people have actually come to impose upon themselves the kind of discipline needed to beget only as many children as they can feed and house and bring up benignly. It is the way described by Peter Bauer: help them, or even just permit them, to attain to a bit of wealth—property they can call their own, or money in the bank, and a situation that offers them some hope of getting more. But this is precisely what Ehrlich and Co. would have the world, for the sake of its future well-being, abjure.

As an old Yiddish expression has it, here is where the dog lies buried: without the threat of world disaster, people privileged to live on a high standard might one way or another, whether unintentionally or in conscious aid of expanding business, help others to acquire this same standard, with its unfortunate concomitant freedoms, all over the world. The problem is not the resources at all—which wealth, in fact, helps to preserve and protect. (Moreover, many of the resources whose depletion most concerns ZPG et al. were not resources at all until men made them so; who knows what might or might not be a "resource" in the future?) No, as Ehrlich himself said, the issue is control, not of the birth rate but of society itself. This sentiment has been widely shared among heads of state in the Third World, who, while they attend conferences and sign statements demanding in effect that the United States *do something* to stabilize the world's population, have not shown themselves notably eager to disperse whatever wealth comes their way to their fellow countrymen who might use it to limit their own families.

In forcing Chinese families to restrict themselves to one child (which has led not only to high rates of abortion but also, according to widespread reports, to female infanticide), the Chinese authorities have really come close to having the right idea, as far as ZPG is concerned. Garrett Hardin would be a drop kinder than they, for in the society governed by his new ethics, families would face just one restriction on childbearing: no more than one girl child per woman. Hardin also has a solution to a problem that the authorities in China may not yet have foreseen. To the extent that they succeed with their policy, they may one day be faced with a plethora of males. This is a problem that many societies, albeit on a rather smaller scale, have been forced to face before, often with unpleasant consequences. Hardin's answer: polyandry (multiple husbands).

Back to the Farm

In the new-ethics polyandrous society, we would, it is true, have to give up a few personal freedoms, but Hardin's associate Ehrlich hastens to assure us that the gains would be great. We Americans would learn to lead more enjoyable and relaxed lives, going back to handcrafts and small farming, which besides making life easier would also help to solve the unemployment problem.

It seems unbelievable that a proposal to return to subsistence farming should be seen as a boon to society. Indeed, it seems unbelievable that a set of ideas so callow, so disconnected from human experience, should ever have been taken seriously at all. And it seems now in hindsight that the proposal might have been greeted with the laughter it deserves were it not for the already lethal condition of the cultural ground in which it took root. The poisons in that ground were themselves contradictory ones, namely, the anarchy of free sex plus the belief that something called "society" was responsible for everything in life. The noxious fumes from this clashing of poisons led to an explosion of passivity combined with mindless rage and self-hatred that for a time nearly did in a generation of America's most advantaged kids and has certainly come near to destroying two generations of disadvantaged ones. A young man declared in the pages of *Esquire* that if he thought he would end up like his father, with a job, a nice house, and kids to support, he would slit his throat. In New York City the so-called moderate feminists stormed down the street demanding the legalization of abortion, on the grounds that a woman had the right to the control of her own body, and when the New York legislature gave it to them, they stormed down the street demanding that abortion be free and available on demand. No matter how much society, especially the government, gave in to their demands, these angry young women still could find no satisfactory settlement between what they were being taught to regard as their desires and the actual constitution of their being. Meanwhile, young men were proudly sporting ZPG lapel buttons announcing that to save the planet they had undergone vasectomy. No wonder every harebrained therapy anyone could devise found a complement of patients. In such a climate, friendly chat from the likes of Paul Ehrlich on how pleasant it will be to give up our freedom and live reduced lives may have sounded quite soothing.

Eventually, as we have lately had ample opportunity to witness, young women of the middle class did find a way to say no to casual sex. Many of them still seem to be somewhat out of sorts, and their various demands on society have not much quieted, but at least the poison of sexual anarchy has been rapidly draining from their systems. Nor are they so cavalier about pushing the idea that motherhood is merely an "option." Now they must face the young men who once so willingly accommodated their anti-natalism, and we can only wonder about what kind of explosion we will witness next.

The Real Victims

But the true victims of that polluted soil remain in our midst. They are the boys and girls of the underclass—blacks in particular—who, having had no margin of the kind provided by the middle class to its young in which to play around with their lives, are left behind with the detritus of those ideas of yesteryear. They, too, boys and girls together, are angry, but this time the community that has long put up with their anger seems less of a mind to excuse it, and there are no loving arms for them to come home to.

Among the things they are doing out there knee-deep in the poison is breeding babies that too many of them have little time or use for. Except for the girls' passivity in the face of what their lives are becoming, they would be perfect targets for Planned Parenthood and the abortionists. So far they are not, because so far the process is still voluntary, and, for whatever reasons, most of them still just go along having the babies, and becoming grandmothers at thirty. But the population controllers, like the famous nine-lived cat, are surely gathering force for yet another rebirth. The opportunity is ripe. For the girls of the underclass, abortion, or at least contraception, may not long remain voluntary. First they will be *bribed* to use Norplant. Should the bribery not take—which seems likely, because why would a few dollars overcome a sloth so profound they permit themselves to be destroyed by it?—they may be forced to do so. America, in short, will have become the land of Francis Galton's dream.

Peter Bauer would know what to tell those kids: Go to work, and save, and be responsible enough to become self-sufficient; then work some more, and quit listening to anyone who preaches to you about either the government or the racists—you don't need to depend on either—and you will see how soon you will begin to prize your babies and how soon after that they will be prizable. Of course, they would not listen to Peter Bauer; things have gotten much too corrupted for that. But they might listen if it were Faye Wattleton or Marian Wright Edelman or Spike Lee or some rap star: any of the people who have achieved their own success and might care enough for these objects of their ideological benefactions—soon otherwise to become the objects of this decade's Francis Galton—to explain the real truth of how you go about it.

Meanwhile, the compulsion to be godlike, and the enormities that follow from it, we may expect to have around in one form or another for quite a while. William Hazlitt, the great British essayist, might easily have had the population controllers in all their various guises in mind when he wrote, in *A Reply to the "Essay on Population" by the Rev. T. R. Malthus:*

It is astonishing, what a propensity Mr. Malthus has to try experiments, if there is any mischief to be done by them. He has a perfect horror of experiments that are to be tried on the higher qualities of our nature, from which any great, unmixed, and general good is to be expected. But in proportion as the end is low, and the means base, he acquires confidence, his tremours forsake him and he approaches boldly to the task with nerves of iron.

2

The Premises of Population Policy: A Reexamination

Nicholas Eberstadt

In recent years the poorer regions of the earth have been swept by a "population revolution" that, while attracting comparatively little international attention, is pregnant with consequences for the peoples of the countries affected. This historically unprecedented "population revolution" has occurred not in the bedrooms, or in the health clinics, but rather in the corridors of government. Among otherwise diverse countries in Africa, Asia, and Latin America, the notion has rapidly gained currency that a modern government should have a "population policy": an array of laws and measures aimed at shaping the composition, size, and rates of change of the national population.

India was the first "Third World" state to establish an active population policy. In December 1952, the Indian government adopted its first Five Year Plan, establishing as a long-run objective the direction of the country's population toward "a level consistent with the requirements of the national economy."[1] By the mid-1980s, more than thirty governments in the less developed regions of the world were implementing "population policy" featuring specific "targets" for fer-

Nicholas Eberstadt is a visiting scholar at the American Enterprise Institute in Washington, D.C., and a visiting fellow at the Harvard Center for Population and Development Studies.

tility and growth rates.[2] Among the thirty were the governments of six of the world's ten most populous countries. By the late 1980s, more than seventy of the world's governments reported that they viewed their national fertility or population growth rates as "unsatisfactory," and that they considered policy interventions to alter these rates "appropriate." As of 1988, more than three billion people lived under such governments: over four-fifths of the population of the less developed regions of the earth at the time, and nearly two-thirds of the population of the entire globe.[3]

The comprehensive "population policy" marks an eventful change in the conception of the role of government. In the past, governments were often called upon to perform duties with demonstrable demographic consequences—to regulate immigration, for example, and to control communicable disease. The demographic impact of such programs, however, was typically subsidiary to their intended purpose, such as the preservation of national sovereignty or the promotion of public health. The idea of harnessing state power to the goal of altering the demographic rhythms of society *per se* suggests—and indeed almost seems to require—a new sort of relationship between the state and the citizen.

The nature of this new relationship is indicated by some of the targets that have been set. The government of Bangladesh, for example, has espoused the goal of a total fertility rate of 2.34 births per family by the year 2000; the current average is believed to be just under 5.[4] The government of Ghana has determined that by 2000 its national fertility rate should be 3.3 births per family, though the current average is thought to be about 6. To meet their targets, both governments would have to oversee a reduction in their people's fertility of roughly 50 percent within just a few years—and in Ghana there are as yet no indications of sustained fertility decline.

Just how such a radical alteration of personal behavior in so intimate a sphere is to be achieved is not clear to outside observers; it may not be clear to those who set the population targets either. But it obviously implies direct, far-reaching, and even forceful state interventions into the daily lives of the overwhelming majority of the citizens of these two countries, and of others with similar targets.

What accounts for the rise of "population policy"? "Population planning" as currently practiced in China—with its "birth quotas" and its manifold pressures and penalties to "convince" parents to have only one child—may seem particularly consonant with the philosophical underpinnings of a Communist dictatorship; yet a stringent and encompassing population policy only somewhat less ambitious than Beijing's has also been executed in Singapore, a society with a nominally democratic government. Indeed, the list of Third World governments committed to shaping the demographic pattern of their societies seems to cover the political spectrum, from dictatorships and one-party states (Haiti, Indonesia) to monarchies (Morocco, Nepal) to genuine constitutional democracies (such as Barbados and Botswana).

The revolution in government presaged by an activist population policy seems therefore to be based less in politics than in "science," for in the final analysis it is the field known as "population studies" that gives population policy its reason to exist. This field of learning, it is widely believed, has advanced sufficiently to permit meaningful predictions of the impact of population changes on the social and economic development of both rich and poor societies. Therefore, since modern governance is based on the idea that national directorates should act to improve the material well-being of their subjects, it should not be surprising that governments see merit in shaping the demographic contours of their country so that national welfare and social prosperity might be "scientifically" advanced.

RELATING POPULATION AND DEVELOPMENT

Unfortunately for all involved, contemporary population policies have been promoted and adopted in large part on the basis of a serious misconception. The relationship between population change and economic development is, notwithstanding bold assertions to the contrary, as yet rather poorly understood. Many of the relationships that have been suggested are at best highly tentative, and cannot be construed to imply causation. Others betray a false precision or misplaced specificity. And despite the authority that "population scientists" today lend to the worldwide effort to promote birth control, convincing evidence that *voluntary* family-planning programs have resulted in sustained changes in fertility norms is still lacking.

The relationship between population change and social or economic change is an awesomely complex topic, one that involves matters of deep personal conviction. Any discourse on population issues may easily touch upon, if only implicitly, the nature of free will, the equality of man, the rights of the living and the unborn, the obligation of the individual to his group, his society, or his God, the sanctity of the family, society's duties to the poor, the destiny of one's nation or race, the prospects for mankind, and the value of life. Such questions are addressed most satisfactorily in consultation with conscience, creed, or ideology. Thus the element of faith, whether directly expressed or inadvertently demonstrated, influences the analysis of "population problems." Although ostensibly secular, population studies often exhibit many of the trappings associated with religious movements.

In recent decades, much of the most influential thinking on the "population question" has taken on a messianic tone. Respected authorities have invoked the image of an apocalypse brought on mankind by adverse population trends, and have justified particular programs requiring great sacrifice or exertion as necessary to stave off hideous alternatives. In 1992, for example, the U.N. Population Fund (UNFPA, from the former name U.N. Fund for Population Activities) announced that "a sustained and concerted program starting immediately" to curb worldwide population growth was essential, since current trends, in the words of UNFPA's director general, create a "crisis [that] heightens the risk of future economic and ecological catastrophes."[5]

Such warnings have been issued before. Stanford University's Paul Ehrlich began his 1968 bestseller *The Population Bomb* with a prophecy: "The battle to feed all of humanity is over. In the 1970s the world will undergo famines—hundreds of millions of people will starve to death in spite of any crash programs embarked upon now."[6] The most optimistic of Professor Ehrlich's "scenarios," involving a radical worldwide program of population control and resource conservation to reduce the world's total population to 1.5 billion (less than a third of its present level) in some future century, nevertheless envisioned the death by starvation of about a fifth of the people alive in the world in 1968. By the same token, *The Limits to Growth,* the 1972 million-selling computer-modeling study sponsored by the Club of Rome, produced a simulation of future trends that suggested an impending "collapse" of global population—proportionately more devastating than the Black Death in medieval Europe—in the absence of a balancing of world birth and death rates by 1975, cutbacks in pollution, and substantial increases in industrial and agricultural efficiency.[7]

Belief in such visions was not always diminished when predictions based upon them were decisively disproven by events. Instead, it often seemed that "demographic believers," like forecasters of the millennium, simply reformulated their prophecies so that they could not be empirically disproven.

Rapid population growth is not the only demographic phenomenon to prompt visions of catastrophe. Dire results have been just as assuredly ascribed to population slowdown or decline. Less than fifty years ago, noted economists like John Maynard Keynes and Gunnar Myrdal (later a Nobel laureate in economics) warned that the failure of Western populations to reproduce themselves would contribute to unemployment, insufficiency of investment, agricultural crisis, and low living standards—precisely the problems that a more recent generation of population experts have described as consequences of rapid population growth!

The tendency to invest in population theories an almost religious zeal, or to harness them to the service of political movements buoyed by public hysteria, might be considerably reduced if there were a body of knowledge that could explain population change, or connect it predictively with various causes or effects. Unfortunately, such a broad understanding of the process of population change does not exist. Although the post-war field of "population studies" has produced wide-ranging, detailed, and often ingenious academic investigations of the interplay between population, economy, and society, nothing like a generalized understanding of the socio-economic causes or effects of population change can be found today, nor does such a thing appear to be in the offing.

It is, of course, almost certainly asking too much of demographers to expect them to provide any overarching "laws of population." No one would demand of a historian a unified "theory of history." The study of human population, for all the mathematical rigor in some of its investigations, is a field of social inquiry, not a natural science. Such relationships as it may uncover at given times in diverse locales are shaped, like all social phenomena, by human values and volition, factors that seldom may be reduced to parameters.

Limits of Population Projections

It is instructive to consider some of the limits of today's "population science." Despite the sophistication of population mathematics, it is impossible to predict the rate of growth of human populations with any accuracy over any extended period of time.[8] Population projections from the fairly recent past highlight the problem. In the 1920s Raymond Pearl, then one of America's leading population biologists, predicted that the United States would reach a population of 200 million around the start of the twenty-second century; in actuality, America passed the 200 million mark in the 1960s. In the 1930s, France's foremost demographers agreed that French population was certain to fall; various projections indicated a drop of between 2 and 12 million people—that is, from 5 to 30 percent—between 1930 and 1980.[9] In actuality, despite the losses it sustained in the Second World War, France's population *rose* by about 30 percent over that period. More recent refinements of techniques have added little to the precision of demographic forecasts. In 1959, for example, the United Nations' medium variant projection put India's 1981 population at 603 million—an estimate that, twenty-two years later, turned out to be off by about 100 million! Long-term population projections can only be right by chance, for there is no scientific method of predicting either death rates or birth rates in the future.

There is reason, moreover, to expect population projections to become *less* accurate in the future than they have been in the past. Advances in public health and public administration now enable governments in low-income regions to reduce national mortality at an increasingly rapid pace—if they are resolved to pursue the required policies, even in the absence of more general social advance. At the same time, the speed with which fertility may change has been increasing. In England and Wales, it took almost eighty years in the nineteenth and early twentieth century for the birth rate to fall by 15 points. In the People's Republic of China in the 1970s, a reduction in the national birth rate of about 20 points was accomplished—by whatever means—in a single decade. Even without aggressively anti-natalist measures, a drop in birth rates of over 15 points occurred in post-war Japan in ten years (1948-1958). With a growing potential for the rapid alteration of demographic trends, the horizon of accuracy in population projections, far from extending, may be drawing ever closer.

One reason why long- and even medium-range population projections are of such limited accuracy is that there is no way to predict fertility change in contemporary societies. There is, in fact, no way to predict even the *onset* of fertility decline in those societies where birth rates are high and seemingly stable. The search for social or economic determinants or preconditions for fertility change has proved frustrating, for societies of the modern world and the recorded past exhibit a breathtaking diversity of relationships between demographic, economic, and social conditions. Low fertility, for example, is commonly thought to be associated with high levels of health; yet life expectancy in contemporary Kenya, where the total number of births per woman is believed to hover around 6.5, appears to be that of Germany in the mid-1920s, where the fertility rate was only 2.3. Fertility decline in nineteenth-century France proceeded even when levels of national mortality were considerably higher than those prevailing in Bangladesh today; by contrast, there is no indication of fertility decline in Oman, whose birth rate is thought to be 30 percent higher, and its life expectancy nearly thirty years greater, than that of France in 1830. Fertility and income are said to be negatively correlated, but the limits of such generalizations are suggested by the World Bank's 1993 *World Development Report,* wherein Tajikstan's per capita output *and* its birth rate are both shown to be about twice as high as Sri Lanka's.[10]

The great diversity of relationships that may be seen between demographic and social or economic conditions makes almost any simple generalization about populations and development hazardous, for there is almost always at least one example that calls the generalized relationship into question. As the historian Charles Tilly observed in a study of fertility, "the problem is that we have too many explanations which are individually plausible in general terms which contradict each other to some degree, and which fail to fit some significant part of the facts."[11]

Practical Problems in Population Studies

If there are broad difficulties with population theories, there are also *practical* problems in the study of population and development. Foremost among these is the problem of false precision. In the statistical accounts used most frequently for the analysis of world demographic and economic conditions, numbers and trends are often presented with a degree of implied specificity that is unwarranted, given the margins of error surrounding them. Not surprisingly, this has often led scholars to erroneous or untenable conclusions.

The nature of the problem is suggested by the 1985 edition of the World Bank's *World Development Report,* the most widely circulated annual publication on development issues. In its statistical appendix, it gives as an estimate for the population of Somalia 5.1 million, with an implied margin of error of 100,000, or about 2 percent. The same appendix gives Somalia a birth rate of fifty per thousand for both 1965 and 1983, again implying a 2 percent margin of error. But Somalia has no registration system for births whatsoever, and as of 1985 had never conducted a national census. Those figures for Somalia were essentially guesses dignified with decimal points.[12]

Somalia, of course, is an extreme example. But the point stands: it is unwise to exaggerate the precision of current demographic estimates. Near-complete vital-registration systems cover only about a tenth of the population of the "Third World"—and tend to be least comprehensive in countries where the connection between population and development is of the most pressing humanitarian concern.[13] Consider also the lag time between the estimated peaking of world population growth and the announcement of it by demographers. It is now widely believed that the world rate of natural increase reached its maximum between 1960 and 1965, and has declined since then. Not until 1977, however, did demographers begin to suggest with any confidence that the peak might have occurred.

If demographic trends are beset by some uncertainties, the estimation of economic output must be an even more tentative matter, involving as it does the measurement not only of populations but also of their per capita production and consumption of goods and services —and the valuation of these things. For less developed countries the problems of estimating levels of economic output and their rates of change can be arresting. To cite but one of many possible examples: a team lead by Irving Kravis of the University of Pennsylvania concluded that India's nominal Gross Domestic Product per capita for 1970 would have been tripled had it been measured, not in dollars at the prevailing rupee-dollar exchange rate, but in terms of the standard international costs of the goods and services the "average" Indian produced. Kravis's purchasing-power adjustments, however, did not affect all poor countries equally. Measured by the regular exchange-rate method, 1970 per capita GDP appeared to be 44 percent higher in Kenya than in India, but after adjusting for differences in actual purchasing power, the Kravis team concluded that the Kenyan per capita GDP was almost 9 percent *lower* than India's.[14] The effect of such adjustments on any presumed correlation between demographic and economic levels in the two countries would clearly be profound.

Population change itself further compounds the difficulty of measuring a society's economic welfare. Because children tend to consume less—often substantially less—than adults, standards of living at any given level of national income can be significantly affected by the age composition of a population. A rapidly growing population in which the average age is comparatively low will appear to have a lower per capita level of consumption than a stationary population with a higher average age, even if at every single age people in both populations consume exactly the same amount. And changes in mortality can introduce even greater biases.

Innovations in public health during this century have typically had their greatest effect on the mortality of children and on diseases associated with poverty.[15] If poorer parents tend to have more children than richer parents, as is the case in many (but not all) low-income societies today, health innovations could seem to be *lowering* per capita income and contributing to greater income inequalities in the society as a whole, even though the families affected by these life-saving changes could judge themselves indisputably better off.

Dan Usher, an economist at Queen's University in Canada, has attempted to impute an economic value to improvements in life expectancy in several developed and less developed countries.[16] Although his results are sensitive to his assumptions about interest rates and the value of additional consumption, they are nonetheless interesting. By Usher's computations, adjustments to account for the value of lengthened lifespans to those whose lives were extended would have raised the nominal annual economic growth rate for Chile for the years 1931-1971 by over half, and would have more than doubled Sri Lanka's for 1946-1968. These may be extreme cases: health improvements in both societies were rapid during those years, and measured rates of economic growth were comparatively slow. Nevertheless, Usher's computations suggest some of the factors that are ignored in conventional discussions of the impact of population growth on a society and its economy—and the effect that ignoring such factors may have on the evaluation of the consequences of population change.

What Is "Overpopulation"?

In the less developed countries of Asia, Africa, and Latin America, governmental concern with the possible adverse effects of population trends today focuses chiefly on rapid population growth. The justification for an activist population policy in those regions is, typically, the need to prevent "overpopulation." But this presents a major problem: there is no workable demographic definition of "overpopulation." The term, though often used as if it had a fixed meaning, cannot be described unambiguously through reference to any combination of demographic variables.

Consider some of the possible demographic criteria by which to judge a society "overpopulated." Is it one in which the *rate of natural increase*—the birth rate minus the death rate—is "unusually" high? If so, the United States in the first decade of its independence was almost certainly overpopulated: between 1790 and 1800 the population grew 3 percent per year—a rate significantly higher than that ascribed to Bangladesh today, and roughly half again as high as the rates currently estimated for Haiti or India. As for a high birth rate: the U.S. birth rate in the 1790s was about fifty-five per thousand—a rate higher than any of the 127 national birth rate "estimates" the World Bank gives in its *World Development Report 1993*, and at least 25 points higher than the estimates for India, Indonesia, and the Philippines.

Perhaps instead overpopulation should be judged by a country's *population density*: its ratio of people to land area. In that case, taking the United Nations figures for 1991, if the Indonesian archipelago was overpopulated, France was more so; if India was overpopulated, Japan was much more so; if Bangladesh was overpopulated, Singapore (where government policy is now striving to *raise* the birth rate) was vastly more so; and by far the most overpopulated state on earth would have been the Kingdom of Monaco![17] Perhaps a high *dependence ratio* —the proportion of children under fifteen and adults over sixty-five in the population in relation to those of working age—may be taken as the criterion of overpopulation. But according to U.N. figures, in 1960 Ireland and Nepal had approximately the same dependence ratio; in 1980 Israel's rate was higher than Sri Lanka's; and the lowest ratios in the world in 1990 belonged to Singapore and Hong Kong.[18]

If *emigration* is the measure of overpopulation, then Mozambique, Angola, and the other "front line" states adjacent to the Republic of South Africa would be overpopulated, while South Africa, which is said to employ more than one million migrants from neighboring nations, would presumably be underpopulated; by the same token, the former East Germany, whose loss of citizens to West Germany proceeded with alacrity until the construction of the Berlin Wall, would have been an overpopulated nation, notwithstanding its government's continual complaints about a labor shortage. Finally, if overpopulation is indicated by *unemployment* (not, strictly speaking, a demographic measure, but one that is often used as such), it would seem that the United States experienced serious overpopulation during the Depression (when fertility fell below replacement levels), and was least overpopulated in the mid-1960s (the years directly following the post-war "baby boom").

Not Overpopulation But Deprivation

"Overpopulation" is a problem, but it is one that is often misidentified. In a more careful discussion, the phenomena most often cited as proof of overpopulation would be seen instead as characteristics of *poverty.* Inadequate incomes, poor health, malnutrition, overcrowded housing, unemployment—images such as these are conjured up by the notion of overpopulation, but they are really images of poverty and material deprivation, conditions that cause great suffering in the modern world.

The actions of government can do much to alleviate material poverty directly, and can do still more to provide an atmosphere conducive to broad-based social and material advance. But it is a profound error to mistake the great range of social and economic problems experienced by human beings for "population problems" driven or created by demographic forces. Rapid population growth is a pervasive fact of life in less developed countries today—a form of social change so typical, and at the same time so profound, that it may be spuriously associated with almost any other current social phenomenon. Many of the problems typically ascribed to "population pressures" turn out upon closer examination to be caused by factors that are independent of demographic trends. In many others the impact of demographic change is, at best, secondary. Social or economic difficulties caused principally by ill-advised or injurious governmental policies are not infrequently misidentified as "population problems" in the modern world. Attempts to redress these problems through activist population programs have all too often made it harder for broad groups and even entire national populations to maintain or improve their standard of living in the face of a hostile political or economic environment.

As we have seen, something like four-fifths of the people of the "Third World" live under governments that have population policies —programs to shape the demographic rhythms of society—and considerable political energy and financial resources are expended on these programs. By the early 1990s, Western governments and Western-funded multilateral organizations were spending over $1 billion a year on population programs in Third World countries. In some countries, such as Bangladesh, the budget for family planning by the 1980s was larger than the budget for all other health-related services combined. What do these family-planning programs and national "population policies" actually do? What is their demographic impact, and how do they affect living standards and development prospects?

Voluntary family-planning programs typically subsidize and promote the use of modern contraceptive technologies by sexually active couples (usually but not always partners in marriage). Modern contraceptives are more effective than such traditional methods of birth control as coitus interruptus, the rhythm method, or the local contraceptive potion. A cheap and readily available supply of modern contraceptives enables parents to improve their own level of comfort, and may, by facilitating the spacing of births, improve the chances for child survival, even if it has no ultimate effect on the size of the family. Such services would be seen as raising living standards today (albeit in ways whose benefits are not easily computed), and might even improve prospects for material progress by augmenting society's stock of "human capital."

Government-sponsored voluntary family-planning programs, under these circumstances, could best be justified as a public-health service, one of the many activities a government may undertake to reduce mortality, augment "human capital," and improve the well-being of individuals and families. Unfortunately, many contemporary advocates of family-planning programs for the "Third World"—both decision-makers in local capitals and enthusiasts from Western countries—have asked for much more: they wish to see voluntary family planning as a technique for reducing fertility in societies where family size is large. The hope is misplaced.

Planning Versus Reducing Family Size

As long as family planning is voluntary, it will remain a tool by which parents may attempt to attain the family size they desire. No research yet conducted has suggested that the advent of modern contraceptives *intrinsically* alters parents' view of children, or ideals about the family. For this reason, similar contraceptive use may be associated with very different levels of fertility.

By World Bank "estimates," 56 percent of the married women of reproductive age in Japan around 1989 used modern methods of contraception (such as the pill, IUD, diaphragm, and sterilization), and Japan's fertility rate for 1991 was 1.5 births per woman. In Turkey, where the usage rate is estimated at 63 percent, the fertility rate is said to be 3.4 births per woman—over twice the level in Japan.[19] That difference speaks, not to the ineffectiveness of Turkish contraceptives, but to the decisive importance of the attitudes and intentions of the people who use them.

The introduction of inexpensive contraceptive methods will, in many localities, result in a decline in "unwanted" pregnancies. But there is no reason to expect that such a decline would always be substantial. Moreover, reducing "unwanted" pregnancies would have less of an effect on population increase than on fertility, since mortality among the unwanted births that would otherwise have occurred would be higher than average. And unless the very availability of modern contraceptives by itself stimulates a revolution in attitudes toward family size—as over a quarter of a century of family-planning efforts has failed to do in Nepal, and three decades of programs have not done in rural Pakistan—the demographic impact of family planning would be a discrete and self-extinguishing adjustment, as the previously "unmet demand" is progressively satisfied.

In many parts of the globe, an effective family-planning program might actually *increase* the birth rate, and the rate of population growth. In much of sub-Saharan Africa, for example, there is little demonstrated interest in modern contraception, but considerable concern about *infertility*. In those societies, the fate of a barren woman is unenviable. Helping parents attain their desired numbers of children might well result in heightened fertility in such circumstances. The example of post-war Kenya, where the fertility rate rose from about six to about eight during a generation of substantial improvements in health, and despite nearly twenty years of family-planning efforts, should make it clear that increasing parents' freedom to choose will primarily serve the purposes of *parents,* whether or not these are in accordance with the goals of the government and its advisers.

The underlying thrust of most family-planning efforts undertaken in less developed countries over the past generation has been strongly anti-natalist, and anti-natalist premises continue to be explicitly enunciated by the principal international institutions funding these efforts, including the World Bank and the U.S. Agency for International Development. These strong sentiments have affected not only the allocation of public funds but also the evaluation of performance.

In a number of less developed countries, the commitment of public funds to family-planning efforts is striking. In 1980, by the World Bank's estimate, the government expenditure per current contraceptive user was $68 in Ghana and $69 in Nepal. These figures compare with World Bank numbers suggesting that the total governmental expenditure on *all* health programs worked out to be about $20 per family in Ghana and $8 in Nepal, in the same year. In such environs, where general levels of mortality are high and health problems are pressing, family-planning programs seem not to be subject to the same strict criteria in competing for scarce funds that other health programs must meet. Family planning's exemption from the ordinary pressures of budgetary finance may be due to a faith that family planning provides additional "services"—such as lowering the birth rate.

The unscientific faith that proponents of family planning have placed in the effectiveness of their programs is suggested by the lack of careful investigations into the actual effects of family-planning projects in trial areas. Although billions of dollars are being expended annually on family-planning services in less developed countries, and such programs have been promoted by various governments for four decades, only a relative handful of studies have attempted to measure the impact of family planning against a "control group"—a similar area that lacks the service.

Measuring the "Unmet Need"

Some proponents of family-planning programs have argued that there is an enormous "unmet need" (as distinct from "unmet demand") for family-planning services in less developed countries. Meeting the need would, by their estimates, require substantially greater funding than these family-planning programs currently receive. Perhaps these advocates are correct, but if so it is not because of the strength of their analysis. Their method of computing "unmet need" is, typically, to measure by sample questionnaire the fraction of women in various societies who say they want no more children or wish to delay birth of their next child, and who also say they are not using modern means of contraception. It is by no means clear that this method measures either the unmet demand for modern contraceptives, or the fraction of the female population exposed to unwanted pregnancy. Women not using modern contraceptives may be practicing traditional (albeit less pleasant or less effective) means of birth control.

Western fertility questionnaires, moreover, have a mixed record in eliciting accurate responses from poor people in less developed societies. Sometimes illiterate villagers, whether in deference or politeness, attempt to please their interrogator with their answers. Moreover, most fertility questionnaires are devoted exclusively to the responses of women, even in areas where the tradition of male dominance invests much of the power of decision with husbands, or even fathers-in-law. Other aspects of such questionnaires may probe into areas of interest to the interviewer but of limited intuitive meaning to the respondent: thus, in some societies canvassed by the World Fertility Survey, over a third of the fecund women who indicated that they wanted no more children also said they would like to have a larger number than they presently had. As a result of such problems, returns from fixed-form, rapidly conducted questionnaires are not always stable: a major survey in Indonesia, for example, found that less than half the women interviewed gave the same figure for "ideal family size" when they were re-questioned four months later.[20]

In Taiwan, Korea, and Hong Kong, family-planning programs have been widely credited with bringing birth rates down. But fertility decline was under way in these places before their family-planning programs were established. In India, by contrast, a national fertility decline did not become unmistakable until decades after adoption of the national planning program; advocates were therefore able to ascribe *all* change in fertility to the government's birth-control efforts. In still other countries, examples being Mexico and Thailand, the establishment of family-planning programs coincided with the start of rapid fertility decline. Yet it is not clear whether the "success" of such programs was due to the government's commitment to push for contraception, or to a change in national attitudes toward family size and fertility decisions (which may have prompted the establishment of the programs in the first place).

In a growing number of countries, governments seem unsatisfied with the family choices that parents have been making and have taken steps to try to change patterns of childbearing. The chosen instruments for altering fertility have ranged from "communications" campaigns of information, propaganda, and exhortation, to the use of incentives and penalties, to the exercise of legal sanctions against childbearing, to the use of techniques of force against would-be mothers and fathers. Such inducements may or may not succeed in changing fertility patterns, or in bringing birth trends more nearly into consonance with the planners' numerical goals. But to the extent that they enforce involuntary adjustments in people's behavior, they may be seen to reduce—not raise—current standards of living, and to compromise, rather than advance, prospects for development.

CONCLUDING OBSERVATIONS

In the assessment of changes in human numbers and all that these changes seem to imply about the fate of national, ethnic, or local populations, ideology has had a tendency to substitute for judgment, and emotion to overpower caution. It may therefore be appropriate to conclude with a few observations distinguished more by tentativeness than by great wisdom.

First, population change is a form of social change. Although population change has profound implications—it involves, after all, the generation and termination of human life—it seems slow by comparison with other forms of change. A 4 percent population increase is considered extremely rapid, while a price inflation rate of 4 percent is, in most developing countries today, considered slow. Moreover, for all the uncertainties of long-term population forecasting, the likely change in size and composition of a national population can be predicted over the course of the coming calendar year with far greater certainty than can changes in the harvest, the gross national product, the unemployment rate, the foreign-exchange rate, or the demand for any particular product. Population change, like other forms of social change, draws upon the ability of individuals, communities, and governments to manage and to cope. For populations that cope poorly with change, any quickening of its pace—including the pace of demographic change—is likely to prove difficult and perhaps costly. Yet coping with change—or as Nobel laureate in economics Theodore W. Schultz put it, "dealing with disequilibria"[21]—is in itself an integral part of modern economic development. It is a learning process, and it generates real economic returns. To the extent that population change prompts this learning process, it can help to speed material development in a given society.

Second, the form that demographic change has taken in the modern era has typically been both comparatively benign and relatively advantageous for the purposes of economic growth. Worldwide population growth has been propelled principally by falling death rates, which is to say, by rising life expectancy. Rising life expectancy is an indication of improved general levels of health, and is suggestive of other changes in living conditions that promote improved health. Improvements in health, moreover, may help to augment the "human capital" upon which the potential productivity of different populations ultimately rests. Augmenting "human capital" does not assure the acceleration of material advance—that will depend on many other things, including the environment of governmental policies in which human talents are set to work. But improved health, and its handmaidens, may well help to quicken the pace of material advance.

Third, much of the current discourse on the "population problem" seems to assume that preventing the birth of poor people will help to eliminate poverty. This appears to be a fundamental error. Mass affluence is typically associated with great transformations of society, economy, and individual outlook. The role of the family, the status of women, and the patterns of fertility typically change in the course of this transformation. But the extent to which reductions in fertility themselves *stimulate* improvements in human productivity is much less clear, either for given families or for whole societies.

Fourth, while the economic consequences of overall rates of population growth are often ambiguous or obscure, the impact of smaller groups within larger populations on the economic well-being of the whole society, or the impact of differential rates of growth within a national population on prospects for material advance, may be direct and important. As Peter Bauer of the London School of Economics has shown, the contribution of religious or ethnic minorities to innovation or economic advance has often been vastly greater than what would be expected from their numbers.[22] By the same token, conflict between rival groups in a society may be intensified by differences in their net reproduction rates; such differences may have implications for the tenor of civil life or for the composition and character of the national directorate, factors that may play a decisive role in determining the "climate" for development.

Finally, the likelihood of gaining unambiguously positive benefits from a policy devoted to shaping the demographic composition of society seems extremely low. The reasons for this go beyond the fact that it has as yet proved impossible to define consistently the "optimum population" upon which activists' efforts to shape society seem to rest. So far, "population policy" in the less developed countries has often attempted to solve through demographic change social problems whose causes lie in ill-advised or injurious governmental policies. It is a peculiar theory of the "second best" that suggests that people's fertility decisions must be altered because the distortions embraced and inefficient policies promoted by governments are immutable. Yet thinking very similar to this seems to have guided some of the population policies that have been put into effect since World War II.

In principle, this problem could be easily corrected. But even if it were, the notion of an active "population policy" would still present difficulties. Interventions in education, health, housing, regional planning, and other areas may have demographic consequences, but they are justified on other grounds. On what grounds would a policy whose primary aim is to induce demographic change be justified? The acceleration of economic growth is one possibility (although, if current patterns of fertility reveal people's preferences about current and deferred consumption, it is not immediately apparent why such preferences should be ignored or overridden).

A Population Policy for Economic Growth

Consider what an active policy to shape population to the cause of accelerated economic growth would require. One possible justification would be "market failure": the possibility that, through distortions and externalities in the price structure of the economy, parents are encouraged to rear the "wrong" number of children. There are good reasons for overcoming market failures, entirely apart from whatever effect such reforms may have on childbearing. Attacking distortions and externalities directly, furthermore, seems preferable to compounding the distortions through compensatory economic penalties or rewards for additional births. And it would be necessary to ask, in a systematic fashion, whether there would be any reason to assume that, in the absence of distortions and market imperfections, parents would not be able to "price" the birth of their child correctly.

To make the economic case for an active "population policy," population planners would ultimately need to center their arguments on estimates of the economic value of human life. They would have to show, in effect, what the "present value" would be of a child born today, and would also have to show how that "present value" would be changed by altering the size of the baby's cohort of peers, or the cohorts following. This would prove to be an extraordinarily difficult task. Assessing the present value of even a physical investment over the course of its projected life is at best a tentative undertaking. Albert Hirschmann, the eminent economist at the Institute of Advanced Studies, has noted that many of the factors that affect the actual productivity of an investment project are not foreseen in even the most detailed planning exercises.[23] If estimating the present value of non-living things is difficult, how much harder it must be to ascribe a present value to an entity imbued with life!

Long-term economic forecasts are notoriously inaccurate. Japan, Taiwan, and Korea defied all expectations of informed foreign observers in the post-war period, while Argentina and Burma, widely expected to be economic successes after independence, did an equally impressive job of disappointing the experts.[24] It is hard to imagine how a population planner would have accurately assessed the "present value" of a birth in Korea in 1955, much less make confident assertions about how that value would be changed through alterations in the Korean birth rate.

"Population planning" for "development," it seems, is easiest to envision under the assumptions of total technological stasis, absence of social change, and rigid restriction of social choices and alternatives. Yet such assumptions, in themselves, contradict the method of economic development and defeat its purpose, which is, in essence, the extension of human choice.

A Response

Robert Engelman

Nicholas Eberstadt and I approach the legitimacy of population policies from very different perspectives. For Eberstadt, population policy is an intrusion, a restriction on human freedom. The tens of thousands of people, the vast majority of them women, who work in the family-planning field see it as precisely the reverse: a community public-health service that expands freedom and personal options—especially for women, who need it most. Population advocacy, properly conceived and executed, involves the measured application and communication of demographic science to bring the mostly male policy-makers of the world to see the value of population policies and programs. And these, broadly, are government-supported efforts on behalf of women (and, in many cases, men) that should be made for reasons unrelated to population growth but too often are not. The heart of these policies is the provision of the means by which women can safely and reliably control their childbearing, and through that, much of their own destiny and that of their children.

Eberstadt asserts that the onset of population policy is an "eventful change in the conception of the role of government." Compared to what? Governments have increased their reach into every aspect of our lives, but population policy represents, if anything, a libertarian and humanitarian turn in almost every case in which it is applied. In this country, over the past century or more, some states have regulated our very marital, sexual, and reproductive choices—prohibiting us from marrying someone of another race, restricting our sexual behavior and expression, and forcing us to continue unwanted pregnancies. I look in vain for some fundamental fault

Robert Engelman directs the population and environment program of Population Action International, Washington, D.C.

line in government's interest in demography, especially when its interest is expressed in the provision of health services for which there is manifest demand, and which are not provided widely, easily, or cheaply by the free market.

Allow me to quote a few phrases from the preamble to the United States Constitution: ". . . insure domestic tranquillity . . . promote the general welfare, and secure the blessings of liberty to ourselves and our posterity." That last phrase speaks to the surprising foresight of the Founding Fathers. On the margin of an "undeveloped" and thinly populated continent, they designed a form of government that would consider the impact of present policies on future generations.

Eberstadt accepts the premise that "national directorates should act to improve the material well-being of their subjects." I would add that they have every duty to advance the non-material well-being as well, in areas such as health and education. He also deals disproportionately with the idea of national well-being without giving concomitant attention to situations where national well-being and individual well-being may be independent of or even at odds with each other.

In fact, societies since time immemorial have had population policies. Historical anthropology is replete with examples of cultures that tightly controlled their numbers—often through infanticide, but more often through taboos of varying stringency, such as post-partum abstinence or polygyny, which reduces fertility.

When a policy serves multiple purposes, it is difficult to argue solely from its demographic basis or results that it is a departure from tradition. Eberstadt makes much of the idea that family-planning programs may be good for public health but are driven by concerns about demography. I'm not prepared to peg a percentage on these two motivations, and I don't think he can, either. I will note that many Muslim countries do not permit family-planning programs to use demographic language or even to tout the benefits of smaller families. Only information about the health benefits of child spacing is allowed. The vast majority of governments throughout history have been strongly pro-natalist, and the link between socially desired population growth and public-health programs aimed at saving lives has been close ever since God told Adam and Eve to "be fruitful and multiply and subdue the earth."

Where the Policies Are

The "eventful change in the conception of the role of government" that Eberstadt is talking about is all but totally absent in the industrialized world. In these countries there are no population policies, with the possible exception of a vague public call to encourage *more* babies in France and a New-Ageish and very much ignored Dutch government document recommending population stabilization in that country.

Eberstadt goes into considerable detail about how many countries, with diverse political systems, have population policies and programs. We in the population community usually use this point in *our* argument. Industrialized countries do not impose population programs; developing countries ask for help in creating and funding their own programs. At least 70 percent of the country reports for the 1992 Earth Summit mentioned concern about the pressures created by population growth.[1] In recent years the United Nations Population Fund has annually been unable to fill $200 million in country requests for population assistance because it lacks the resources. And in most cases the countries themselves spend far more money than they are given by donors for population activities.

Eberstadt's point is interesting: Since the existence of such policies cannot be explained by politics, it must be based on "science." But this doesn't follow at all. Would that more policies not based on politics *were* based on science! Isn't it more reasonable to expect that common policies stem from common *experience,* that governments the world over have found, especially in recent years, that they simply cannot keep up—while hoping to develop economically—with the educational and health needs of a population that does not have access to modern contraception?

Egypt, with 58 million people now, cannot feed its people; it depends on U.S. gifts of wheat. Egypt is projected to have between 86 million and 101 million people in 2025. What would you do if you were President Mubarak—hope the United States can feed your people forever, no matter what their numbers?

The key variable here is probably not population growth *per se,* but fertility and age structure of a population. When governments are racing to keep pace with ever larger cohorts of elementary school students each year, ever larger cohorts of entrants into the job market, ever larger numbers of restless university students with more political convictions than future prospects—not to mention maternal and child mortality, which is closely linked positively to high fertility and negatively to access to modern contraception—all this tends to concentrate the minds of policy-makers.

Population Growth and Economic Growth

I start with the assumption that the link between economic growth and population is not firmly established. We are dealing with human beings here, not physics or chemistry. And as Eberstadt points out, every country presents a melange of different conditions and experiences. However, most of those who work in the population field or make policy in the area generally accept the link on simple logic, intuition, personal experience—and substantial documented evidence. At some levels the problems inherent in adjusting to ever-larger, ever-younger populations begin to offset the economic benefits derived from that population as a human resource. And I've seen no evidence that in the past decade or so rapid population growth in any country acted in any fashion as a multiplier of the GNP or other independent economic assets.

Let's just look at the world around us. Certainly there is no linear relationship between fertility and economic development. Some of the highest fertility, for one thing, can be found in some of the richest per capita nations: those in the Middle East. Clearly they are an aberration, relatively small populations sitting on large reserves of oil that are in only the early stages of diversifying their economies. Look at the most dynamic economic growth of today, in Japan and the East Asian "tigers," and consider just how the strongest economic growth correlates with fertility. Then let's perform the same exercise with Africa, comparing the two continents. Then consider Latin America. I suggest that with the sole significant exception of the Middle East, there is a close correlation between total fertility rates and economic growth rates. This is not to suggest that one causes the other. But it is noteworthy that a decade or more ago every Asian tiger introduced a government-sponsored family-planning program, which found an immediate market and contributed substantially to rapidly declining fertility.

This connection between population characteristics and economic growth can hardly be said to be overstressed or oversimplified in the press and public consciousness. Population growth rates, not to mention fertility rates, are rarely mentioned in media discussions of national economies around the world. In 1992 the *Washington Post* published an extensive and provocative series comparing the economic success stories of Asia with the economic failures of Africa. Not once was the extreme disparity of the two regions' population growth or fertility rates mentioned.

Eberstadt succumbs to one of the faults he criticizes in others when he asserts that "many of the problems typically ascribed to 'population pressures' turn out upon closer examination to be caused by factors that are independent of demographic trends. In many others the impact of demographic change is, at best, secondary." A surprising precision is implied in these statements. Eberstadt suggests he can convincingly demonstrate factors that not only cause problems within nations but have absolutely nothing to do with demographic trends. And he implies that he can quantify the impact of demography and other unspecified factors to demonstrate which are primary and which are secondary. Perhaps he can do this, but I cannot, and he has not done so in his essay.[2]

Targets, much criticized by Eberstadt, are not in most places as important as he implies. Although the use of targets has definitely led to some abuses, in most cases targets act as general guideposts within rather than outside of bureaucracies. The population community long ago abandoned the term "population control," and governments are coming round as well. The reality is that population cannot be controlled, because people cannot be controlled. Targets—like those that exist in other aspects of health care, in economics, and in business—are in most places little more than the weaponry of unimaginative bureaucracy, designed to inspire the troops rather than actually to control anyone's fertility.

The situation in China certainly cannot be cited in support of the power of voluntary family-planning services. There is very little chance that China is not coercing at least some women to have fewer children than they wish to have. No one I know of in the population community—within the U.S. Agency for International Development or the U.N. Population Fund or anywhere else—has anything less than the strongest condemnation of this coercion. But it is also true that we really don't know its extent. There is so little reliable information that we cannot say whether China's program is systematically coercive or merely vulnerable to locally directed abuses. Partly for this reason, we simply don't know whether to condemn or merely withhold judgment on the spectacular fertility declines in China in recent years. They certainly are not entirely the product of coercion. Improvements in health care generally, in the education and overall status of women, and in the reliability of the contraceptives China uses all undoubtedly play a role. And it's interesting to note that in a *New York Times* article in May 1993 that discussed at length China's family-planning program excesses, Nicholas Kristof reported that a large proportion of the Chinese people were quite supportive of the country's population policies; they believed that China's dramatic reductions in population growth rates were a major factor behind its economic success, particularly in comparison to the populations and economies of South Asia.[3]

Demographic Uncertainties

Fundamentally, our opinions on these matters reflect our values. Certainly there is uncertainty in demography. It's not nearly as bad as Eberstadt portrays it, but there is uncertainty. So what? Is demography more uncertain or less scientific than economics, international relations, or environmental science? I'm not sure how the arguments of population policy advocates are weakened by the fact that we really don't know what population will be in 2050.

It is ironic that every past error of population projection that Eberstadt mentions *underestimated* the population growth that actually occurred. That certainly doesn't inspire confidence that the situation is really less worrisome than population experts warn.

The people who need to hear the message of the uncertainties inherent in population projections are the long-term planners in the World Bank and elsewhere who ponder how many dams we must build and how much food production must be increased by 2050. Most planners take the medium projection of population growth as the most likely one—which it is not—and then inflate it into an "exogenous input"—a given—in their planning. Experience shows there is abundant room for acting to reduce population growth, so that the *lowest* projections begin to resemble prophecies, rather than the higher ones.

If the question were whether to take some onerous policy step to restrict the growth of population immediately, perhaps we in the population community would need to establish an absolutely airtight scientific case that rapid population growth is bad for human development and the future availability of natural resources. But since the policies we are in fact considering have a demonstrated history of improving health and expanding human freedom, we don't need an airtight scientific case—or, indeed, any scientific case at all. All we need to demonstrate is the strong likelihood that expanding access to high-quality family planning is neither expensive nor burdensome, and that it saves the lives of women and children, expands opportunities for women to contribute to their societies economically, culturally, socially, and politically, *and* provides nations with a bit of breathing space to prepare for the population growth that is inevitable.

Similarly, Eberstadt's point about the imprecision of the term "overpopulation" needs no rebuttal. It *is* subjective. I don't know how to define overpopulation, and my organization doesn't use the term. It reflects a judgment in a given situation that "there are too many people," with the implication that some of those people should be gone—an offensive idea to say the least. I don't take the term seriously, nor do I know others within the population community who do.

Population and Cumulative Risks

What I do take seriously is the concept of cumulative and escalating risk. What I mean by this is the kind of one-way megatrends that show no indication of reversing on their own (in fact, many are accelerating), are dominated in the short term by sheer momentum (population growth and human alteration of the atmosphere deserve special mention here), and appear potentially complicating, or hazardous, without any obvious benefits to the world. My experience and judgment tell me that the relationship of population growth to economic and human well-being probably changes with time and with population size. A benefit that may have existed at some point in the past when population sizes and densities were much lower around the world may have disappeared over the past forty years as three billion people have been added to a world that took from the dawn of human time to 1960 to acquire the first three billion.

How does population relate to these cumulative risks? Obviously they reflect consumption, technology, and patterns of living and governing as well. But population growth unquestionably expands the scale of human activity on the planet. Since Eberstadt ignores the critical question of balance between the earth's physical and biological systems and human population, I will address it only by noting its regrettable omission. But if we ever decide that we want to stabilize population, we will have to wait a good two generations after beginning the process, in which time a lot can happen. Despite all the uncertainties of population projections, I can show you curves reflecting population momentum and the very likely course of population size over the next fifteen to twenty years. I can tell, for example, that even under the lowest feasible U.N. population projection, Africa's population almost triples in size in the next century, reaching a size about 40 percent larger than China's current population. Even if tomorrow African women began having no more than two children each—and despite the uncertainties of demographic projection, I can promise you that this will *not* happen tomorrow—the continent's population would rise from the current 650 million to over 1 billion. As Eberstadt points out, we don't really know Somalia's population. That's convenient for me: let's just say that, like the rest of Africa, it triples in size in the next century. Is that likely to make it easier or more difficult for Somalia to solve its many problems?

We don't know. But my experience and simple logic suggest that for a country like Somalia, as for others in Africa, where soil is rapidly degrading, where land is being subdivided into increasingly small parcels that will not support families, where water is increasingly unavailable to women and their children, a tripling of population is far more likely to work *against* human well-being than for it. I look at Haiti, now almost entirely deforested and with poor and rapidly degrading soils, and I ask whether a democratic government will be able to transform the country into a smoothly functioning one along the lines of Costa Rica, and whether the currently high fertility or a lower fertility is more likely to contribute to the kind of development that really improves people's lives.

Unless you believe that the capacity of the earth's resources and waste sinks, as modified perhaps by human imagination and work, is absolutely without limit, you are forced to agree that there is some level of human occupation of the planet at which well-being would decrease with further additions. But in order to stabilize world population size at that number, fertility rates must decline to replacement or below a generation or more before that peak number is reached.

Eberstadt says that a government population policy in Bangladesh and Ghana aimed at reducing fertility by roughly fifty percent by the year 2000 "obviously implies direct, far-reaching and even forceful state interventions into the daily lives of the overwhelming majority of the citizens." He uses the phrase "enforced reductions in fertility" even when speaking about voluntary family planning. If one absolutely rejects coercion, as the vast majority of family-planning programs do, how can voluntary family planning "enforce" reductions in fertility? And how can he explain the evident popularity of family-planning programs in predominantly Catholic countries such as the Philippines, where polls show overwhelming support for President Ramos's policies despite all-out opposition from the Catholic Church? This has been well demonstrated as well in Mexico, Colombia, and Peru, among other Catholic countries. In democracies, population programs that do not maintain public support eventually come back to haunt politicians—as happened to Indira Gandhi in India in the 1970s. Those that survive—now in dozens of countries around the world—must not be terribly intrusive. And indeed, on the face of the evidence they are supplying a service that is very much in demand.[4]

The Crowded Dance Floor

Eberstadt's arguments on the impact of family planning on fertility are artfully worded. I can't be certain that I can contradict his statement that the provision of modern contraceptives does not "*intrinsically* alter parents' view of children, or ideals about the family." I'm not sure what "intrinsically" (the emphasis is his) means here, but it sounds like something of a hedge. There is plentiful survey research demonstrating what demographers sometimes call the "crowded dance floor" phenomenon, whereby family-planning efforts do face initial skepticism and resistance but eventually spark catalytic responses and accelerating demand. The more people practice family planning, the more it becomes accepted, and the more additional women and couples are brought to the practice. Word spreads, despite the profoundly private nature of the activity. Women notice that their neighbors are accomplishing more around the house, on their land, or in their jobs because they gave birth only when they wanted to, rather than when "God" or "fate" determined. This is well documented in the literature, and I have heard testimony too many times and from too many women to doubt the power of the phenomenon.

On infertility, I can only say without hesitation that unwanted infertility should be eliminated wherever possible. I would add that reproductive health care that stresses family planning and the prevention of sexually transmitted disease also reduces infertility. Much of it is caused by adolescent pregnancy or unsafe abortion. I will make a bargain with Eberstadt: if he will join me in making sure that quality voluntary family-planning services are universally available, I will join him in advocating universal availability of infertility-prevention services.

His point about Japan is simply in error, and his use of Turkey is misleading. Women and men in Japan do not have access to a broad choice of modern contraception. The pill is not even approved for contraceptive use there, a policy decision that was reaffirmed in 1993 because of fears that the use of the pill would contribute to the spread of AIDS. The Japanese rely on the condom—and, it should be added, about a million abortions a year in a population less than half the size of our own. I would not disagree that desired family size in Turkey is higher than it is in Japan. I find it grounds for celebration that people with a variety of preferences for family size use contraception. And in a world of universal access to reliable contraception, no doubt fertility disparities will remain because of differences in preference. But the simple fact is that less than half of Turkey's contraceptive use is modern contraceptive use, and I would take issue with Eberstadt's dismissal of the possible "ineffectiveness of Turkish contraceptives."

Eberstadt's figures on government expenditures per contraceptive user are so misleading as to be completely without value. He deftly compares family-planning spending *per contraceptive user,* but health spending *per family.* Given the extremely low contraceptive prevalence in the countries he mentions, these figures don't suggest very high family-planning budgets. With Nepal and Ghana we are also dealing with the establishment of a service infrastructure that scarcely exists in these countries now. Most of Nepal's people live in virtual isolation from the capital of Katmandu; it can take days to reach them. But Eberstadt understands the concept of marginal cost, which plummets as the family-planning infrastructure is developed. The average annual cost per contraceptive user in the developing world is somewhere in the range of $10-25.

His question about the relative expenditures on family planning versus "all" health programs is well taken, however, despite his omission of family planning from his category of "all" health expenditures. (It is uniformly part of a country's health budget and lies within health ministries.) There is a live debate about what this balance should be, and I am not sure how his figures were arrived at. But again, the disparity often depends on timing. Inexpensive preventive-health services are being compared in many cases to the startup of new services that require training, outreach, and infrastructure development. A simple comparison doesn't make sense without more information on what is being compared to what. In some cases, family-planning budgets include the first real extension of *any* preventive health care to women. I don't know if it is true that more is spent on family planning than on the sum total of other health services in these countries. I would suggest that it is among the least expensive of public health services, given its benefits in saving the lives of mothers and children and reducing fertility rates.

Family Planning and Fertility Decline

Eberstadt's point about the lack of evidence that voluntary family planning has resulted in sustained fertility reductions also is simply in error. (His wording is interesting: "*convincing* evidence that voluntary family planning programs have *resulted in sustained* changes in fertility *norms* is still lacking" [my emphasis]. This is a very high standard.) This is one of the most studied areas of modern demography. And while any lively discipline includes debates on such matters, there is not much serious disagreement in the field that access to family-planning services is a critical component—usually an essential component—in fertility decline. Demographer John Bongaarts and colleagues estimated that organized family planning could claim credit

for the avoidance of 412 million births since about 1950 and contributed about 50 percent to the fertility decline the world has seen
since that year.[5] Eberstadt would perhaps argue that this is false precision, and I would agree. Yet this is the figure the body of demographic research converges on.

Here are the relevant figures on contraceptive use and fertility for
Kenya (it should be noted as well that Kenya's economic growth from
1984 to 1993 has been unimpressive, but modern contraceptive prevalence has quadrupled and fertility has declined by a third)[6]:

> 1978: contraceptive prevalence rate (CPR) 7 percent, modern con-
> traceptive rate unknown; total fertility rate (TFR) 8.1 children
> per woman.
> 1984: CPR 17% (modern 7%); TFR 7.7
> 1989: CPR 27% (modern 18%); TFR 6.7
> 1993: CPR 33% (modern 28%); TFR 5.4

Eberstadt suggests that demographic studies based on controls are
few and far between and challenges the conclusion that the availability
of family planning contributes to fertility decline. This will surprise
those demographers—to cite just one example—who have worked
in the Matlab district of Bangladesh. They have found strong correlations between access to family planning and not only fertility but
other indicators of female empowerment with extensive comparisons
to control areas.

Obviously the demographic transitions of Europe were largely accomplished without modern contraception, though Europe had the
benefit of a relatively empty western hemisphere, Africa, and Oceania
to migrate to, as well as strong marital and cultural constraints and
abortion—all of which contribute to fertility decline. In the modern
world it's a real challenge to find a country in which fertility has
declined noticeably but access to modern contraceptive services has
not expanded dramatically. In Thailand, Mexico, Morocco, Zimbab-
we, and Colombia, and—in recent years—in India, Kenya, Nigeria,
Peru, and (of all places) Iran, fertility decline has been accompanied
by expanded access to modern contraception. One can rarely prove
causation in such matters, but the correlations are too impressive to
be coincidental. This is especially so in light of numerous demo-

graphic surveys that at least suggest—bearing in mind Eberstadt's assertion that people in the developing world for some reason are different from the rest of us in telling a survey worker only what she wants to hear—that as reproductive health-care services spread, women begin to think about their *options* in childbearing, and their options in other areas of their lives, in new ways.[7]

Male Opposition to Family Planning

I find astounding the almost parenthetical comment Eberstadt makes about areas where "the tradition of male dominance invests much of the power of decision [in matters of family formation] with husbands, or even fathers-in-law." This is one of the strongest arguments for reaching women with family-planning services. Anyone who values human liberty should ask: Why should women be forced to do the bidding of their husbands or fathers-in-law in giving birth, when it may threaten their health, even their lives, and largely determines their fate? Why should they not be allowed to make their own decisions on such an intimate and fateful matter? And why would not anyone who celebrates human beings as the "ultimate resource" not decry the loss of half of that resource—other than through the indirect but socially valuable service of raising children—to a society's economy, its culture, its political life? Does this not put in perspective Eberstadt's concerns about "coercion" in family-planning programs? Certainly such abuses exist, but just as certainly they are several orders of magnitude less prevalent than the coercion that forces women to bear children they do not ask to have. In fact, the prevalence of male opposition to family planning is probably somewhat exaggerated. But where men seek to control women's fertility, women desperately need contraception that empowers them to make their own decisions on childbearing. And they cry out for it, given a chance and the realization that the possibility exists.

What looks to many people like population *control,* in the worst sense of the term, looks to many women in the developing world like *options* for meeting an increasingly desperate need. The need is increasing because in almost all parts of the developing world, not only fertility but family size preferences are decreasing.

We are *not* imposing some new Western way of doing things on the people of the developing world, certainly not in the way that many would argue we are imposing our model of development on them. What we are doing is completing a revolutionary "imposition" of Western values and technologies in public health that we began over the past century and have so far left incomplete. It was the scientific knowledge and technology of the West that brought sanitation, immunization, better knowledge of nutrition, and the improved crop yields that slashed death rates throughout Africa and the rest of the developing world. It is not increasing fertility but decreasing mortality that has driven the unprecedented population growth of the past four decades. Sustained high fertility coupled with plummeting mortality increasingly burdens traditional institutions and living patterns that evolved for thousands of years under conditions of relatively small and stable populations. *We*—not poverty, not religion, not tradition—have dramatically elevated population growth rates in developing countries and forced the pace of change into overdrive. The least we can do is share with these countries the equally life-saving technology we have developed to enable women and men safely and confidently to decide whether, when, and with whom to bear a child. Eberstadt speaks hopefully of the "learning process" inherent in "'dealing with disequilibria,'" as though population growth itself generated the education so desperately needed in the developing world. But who are we to maximize the disequilibria of societies that are least capable of adjusting to rapid change?

China appears to be the last bastion of true coercion in family-planning service delivery—although we don't know how widespread the practice is—and that fact relates more to the unique aspects of the Chinese system than to any lingering global momentum to force contraception or abortion on women. The reality of coercion is the reverse: all over the world, from the refugee camps of Kenya to the hospitals of Louisiana, women are forced to bear children they did not plan for and do not want. In my value system, the ethical high ground includes the elimination of forced maternity.

The population community stands in near unanimity, with a handful of dissenters who have no influence, that the basis of all legitimate action on population is the free and informed choice by individual women and men of the timing and number of pregnancies and childbirths. Joint decision-making within marriages on such matters should be respected and encouraged. But since women are the ones who bear the children, their choices should take precedence over those of men or family members, which is in most places the absolute reverse of the situation today.

If we can agree, on all sides of this debate, that our goal is to give women the right to bear children when they choose and plan to, then the rest of the debate should be a simple application of eminently testable theories. Mine is that somewhere between a third and a half of all births are to women who did not plan or welcome the pregnancies. If I am wrong, and the proportion is much lower, then I will concede there is not much point in working to improve access to contraception. I will then confine my efforts to reduce population growth to such strategies—important in their own right—as greater access to education, credit, jobs, and political power for women. If I am right, then a very high priority for the world community should be providing universal access to safe, high-quality, voluntary family-planning services.

Comments

Steve Hayward: China presents an extraordinarily difficult problem. I'm reminded of a passage in Leo Strauss's book *On Tyranny:* What would we say about a social science or a political science that couldn't recognize tyranny for what it is? What would we say about a medical science that couldn't recognize cancer for what it is? It seems to me that no matter what opinion you might have on population, we are right to be suspicious of any kind of population-control policy in a regime like China. I was a little troubled by Robert Engelman's appeal for a distinction between what parts are coercive and what parts are not. It seems to me very hard to make such a distinction in that kind of regime.

Robert Engelman: I have full respect for everyone who believes that this is a fundamental question of ethics and morals and should be addressed only, or at least primarily, on that basis. This is perhaps the liveliest and most important debate within the population community also. It is a very, very difficult issue.

Hadley Arkes: What standard do we use to judge what is the desirable level of population? This is a question that those of us who oppose population control don't have to take on, and beyond that, we don't think there is any such number that establishes, in principle, the "right" level of population. Now, if we put that aside, it's clear that we have, in China, a direct violation of personal choice. If you were to say, "Well, some Jews died in the gas chambers and some Jews died natural deaths," we wouldn't say, "Then hold off the judgments; after all, we don't know just how many died in gas chambers." We would say, "We condemn the deaths that occurred in gas chambers." Simi-

---

Note: Participants in this section are identified on pages 161-62.

larly, we might expect you to say, "We condemn the violation of personal choice in China."

Robert Engelman: We absolutely condemn the violation of personal choice.

Hadley Arkes: Then why are you holding off on your judgment about China?

Robert Engelman: Because many women have benefited from the Chinese program. Should we therefore withdraw our support from anything China does if the withdrawal means that more women will die and more will be coerced to have children they do not wish to have? I do not accept the idea that we must universally either condemn China or embrace it. We can condemn the violation of personal choice.

Hadley Arkes: What you are saying is that it's all right to violate personal choice and abridge personal freedom if, in the aggregate, you bring about a situation in which life is enhanced.

Robert Engelman: We condemn the violation of personal choice wherever it occurs. And we also believe in being involved with governments whose programs we do not approve of in every respect, in the hope that we can improve their policies and improve the lives of women. Some people argue that we should not have anything to do with China because of this clear violation of morality. I do not believe that China should be abandoned to do whatever it wants in family planning. My opinion is both that China's coercive measures are a violation of morality and that China should be worked with.

John Aird: I take exception to the suggestion that it is an uncertain question whether coercion is a matter of national policy in the Chinese government's family-planning program. I think it is uncertain only for people who do not examine the evidence. One of my great disappointments, as a professional demographer and a long-time supporter of family planning, is that too many professionals have shown a considerable reluctance to resolve the uncertainty. It seems to me that if they are as deeply concerned as they claim to be about the importance of discouraging coercion, then when cases in which coercion was alleged appear on the international scene, they should feel compelled to delve into the matter as thoroughly as possible.

I'm also a little troubled by the all-or-nothing notion, the idea that the issue with China is, Shall we support everything they're doing while objecting morally to some of the actions, or shall we totally withdraw? It seems to me that we *should not* support activities that involve unacceptable moral or ethical concomitants and *should* support other activities that do not. Coercion runs through the entire family-planning program; it's intrinsic to it. I don't see how you can support any aspect of that program without putting yourself in the position of saying, either that you don't care about the coercive aspects of it, or that you really don't think they are that important, or that you think they are outweighed by the advantages. The all-or-nothing notion does not recognize the finer distinctions that are possible when we are dealing with what we regard as violations of human rights or unethical behavior.

Robert Engelman: I have a feeling that you and I are not terribly far apart on this. China currently does not have a tremendous problem with AIDS, but it certainly has the potential for it—a very great potential, with 1.2 billion people, a very youthful age structure, and high rates of TB infection. Much of the U.N. Population Fund's involvement in China has been to assist in the manufacture of condoms. I think it is very difficult to coerce the use of condoms, and I believe that condoms are very effective in preventing the spread of HIV. What should our policy be in helping China—which has shown very little capacity to develop the technology itself—to get reliable condoms to some hundreds of millions of sexually active young people? I would argue that we should assist China in every way we can to make more and better condoms while at the same time we strongly condemn the coercion in their family-planning program.

John Aird: What the Chinese regime advocates, to virtually everybody, is (1) IUDs for all women with one child, (2) sterilization of either the male or female in couples who have two or more children, and (3) abortion of all unauthorized pregnancies. Now they are also open to the use of the new birth-control implants, which lend themselves to coercive application. They know that you can't coerce the use of condoms. They want what they call "permanent" solutions to the problem. It is clear that the more effective methods are those that are forcibly used. Of course, you can coerce people to do anything if you use certain types of penalties. Even the economy can be a coercive instrument if you inflict heavy economic penalties on the consequences of non-use.

The regime has been promoting the idea that control of population growth is essential, not only to economic development in China, but also to the food supply. Well, the food situation had been improving steadily in China before the family-planning program took hold. It had gotten a lot better except for the big famine years of 1959-61. Then it stultified for a long period of time, until 1980, when the Chinese abandoned the commune system and retrenched on collectivization. By the late 1970s the birth rate, which had begun to fall in 1972, had dropped considerably. But the economic response did not occur in response to the drop in fertility. It occurred after a change in the policy that was dampening motivation for production in both rural and urban areas. The real take-off occurred after the opening of the special economic zones in the late 1980s.

So the prosperity the Chinese economy is showing now seems a more direct response to administrative changes that released individual motivation than to family planning. The whole process was followed by family planning, but not right away. You must beware of stopping the analysis of a complex situation at the point where you get an answer that is favorable to your inclination. Go a little deeper to be sure that the evidence really points only toward that conclusion before you decide.

Jean Guilfoyle: Women in the Third World have a very strong resistance to the American population-control policies. At the World Women's Congress in Miami, in preparation for the 1992 U.N. Earth Summit, Third World women spoke out plainly and courageously. In this country the National Women's Health Network has been performing some very needed research on the negative effects of contraceptives on women.

Robert Engelman: I really do resist the idea of talking about how Third World women feel. I am a First World male, very white, very wealthy in comparison to most people, so I can't begin, myself, to speak for Third World women, but I don't think a First World woman can, either. I also don't think that even Third World women can speak for all of their counterparts. I have been impressed by the wide variety of opinions on contraception and every other political topic under the sun among the many Third World women that I have met. The women who spoke in Miami, for the most part, had levels of income that were massively higher than the income levels of most of the women that I've spent time talking to in the Third World. Certainly their concerns are valid, but I do not think that there is unanimity in the Third World. The popularity of family planning is not in dispute anywhere. It is amazingly popular.

Diarmuid Martin: On the matter of quantifying the unmet need: At the European Population Conference, the draft final declaration referred to a figure of c. 300 million persons who have no access to the family-planning services that they wish to have. I asked for the origin of this figure and was told it was from the UNFPA. The following day the UNFPA issued a correction saying that the figure reflected not 300 million *persons* but 300 million *women* who have unmet needs for contraception. The same day, the United States delegate gave 100 million women as the figure. These are enormous differences. Can you really build policies on such divergent statistics? This argument of the unmet need is coming more and more to the fore. Scientific papers on the subject do exist, and they tend to opt towards the lower level.

Robert Engelman: One of the things that most concern me in this field is the lack of precision. Both sets of numbers come from surveys that have been funded by the U.S. Agency for International Development and others for a period of years: these surveys are very standardized and are of high quality. The 300 million generally refers to the number of couples—it could be applied to either women or couples, the assumption being that they are married or are at least living in union—who do not have access to family planning. We generally use 125 million (maybe somebody used 100 million) as that subset of the 300 million who not only lack access to any type of modern contraception but say that they would like to avoid becoming pregnant or currently have an unwanted pregnancy. The assumption is made that people who respond this way *would* use a contraceptive service if they had access to one. The figure does not include adolescents and women not in a union who may have a need for contraception, so it underestimates real need. It also does not include women who are not using contraception but who *might or might not* use it if it were available and if it were of a certain type. (It's not clear to me how this way of reckoning approaches the natural family-planning method.) So yes, it's subject to much error, but not as much as you might think.

Gilbert Meilaender: In the course of the conversation I've realized that I'm not simply for freedom. Freedom is only one aspect of being human. I'm not for a freedom that thinks it can talk about married women without reference to marital bonds, for example. I myself have raised objections when people who oppose population policies do so simply on the grounds that childbearing is a personal choice that shouldn't be interfered with. I don't think this captures the full reality of the choice. Barbara Katz Rothman, a sociologist, has written about women who get amniocentesis and, because of what this prenatal diagnosis shows, have an abortion. Rothman, who is certainly in favor of abortion, ended up suggesting that women ought not always to seek amniocentesis, that they ought simply to decline to learn certain kinds of information. Her argument was that technology designed to enhance the freedom of women in fact turned out to control women in various ways. It takes on a life of its own, a kind of momentum that is very difficult to resist. What purportedly expands freedom in fact restricts it. I think it is naïve to believe that simply making various kinds of technology available to people in and of itself expands human freedom.

Robert Engelman: We can go too far in saying that women should be the sole decision-makers about their own fertility. There is a fundamental human relationship, one that is sometimes called a sacrament, involved here. It's complicated. Ideally, childbearing is a joint decision, but in a number of societies men either oppose any kind of restriction on fertility or do not communicate well at all with their wives or force their wives to have sex against their wishes or insist on large families and take little or no responsibility for the children.

Technology can be destructive. We must not simply embrace a technology because some scientists have told us it's hot stuff. We love technology, but that is not a reason to justify contraception. Unless a modern means of contraception meets a real and present human need, we ought to look at it with extreme suspicion.

It costs money to buy safe and effective contraceptives. There is a role for governments to facilitate the availability of this technology; but fundamentally, individual people and couples need to choose what makes sense for them, what risk/benefit ratio they want to apply to their own lives. It is our responsibility to make sure that they have the choice and are free to make that choice.

Midge Decter: Technology often has unintended and unforeseeable consequences. We are beginning to see some of the consequences, not so much of contraception, perhaps more of abortion, but primarily of the focus on women in child-rearing. One of the consequences is a growing separation of the man from the child. It's being fostered in part by the abortion argument that "this is my body and I have the right to my own body." This separation of the man from the child enables men to say, "O.K., honey, so long—good luck to you," and walk away. Where I live I see a lot of plucky young women taking their little kids off to the day-care center, being very brave about it; since this has all been given into the woman's keeping, it is very easy for the man involved to say, "O.K., so long." I'm not advocating a policy; I'm just pointing out a consequence of separating men spiritually and emotionally from their families.

The feminists who are demanding family planning for their African sisters in Somalia have in mind that these women should be able to determine their own fate over and against the men who have been brutalizing them and pushing them around. Who am I to say that my African sisters shouldn't have a better chance? On the other hand, when what you are talking about is the manipulation of procreation, you are dealing with extremely dangerous stuff.

Calvin Beisner: On the matter of population projections: In 1969, the U.N. forecast 7.5 billion people in the world in the year 2000.

Five years later the figure was 7.2 billion. One year later it was nearly 7 billion. Less than a year later it was down to at least 5.8 billion, and within the next year, it was down to around 5.4 billion. That's a drop of roughly a third in a twenty-three-year forecasting period during which the majority of the people who would be alive at the end of the forecast were already alive. A margin of error of that magnitude is not only not scientific but also not credible. Nigeria is fairly well known among people who follow these things. In 1992 the first thorough, scientific census count in Nigeria was released, showing a population of about 88 million. Yet the major population tracking organizations—the UNFPA, World Bank, Planned Parenthood, the Population Reference Bureau—had all made estimates that vastly exceeded the census figure. The closest one was 33 per cent high; the average margin of error was 36.9 per cent high. We're talking here about estimates of a *current* population, not about projections. When the figures are that far off, I have a problem believing that there is much science behind how the figures are put together, and I find it disconcerting that all the estimates were off in the same direction.

As for China's capacity to make condoms: twice in 1992-93, after the U.S. president announced a cut in our defense expenditures, the very next day China announced a 10 per cent *increase* in its defense expenditures. It's the old guns-or-condoms question. Do we have to subsidize condoms in China? Couldn't we instead encourage China to reorganize some of its priorities a bit?

John Aird: Over the years demographers have made it abundantly clear that projections simply represent the working out of the assumptions that you have put into them. They are not a prediction. However, it has proved to be an almost impossible message to deliver. I've had this experience many times: people come to demographers to get a number to work with, and they're not interested in the story that goes with it. They want to grab a number and run. There's no way to beat that. When I was making projections, I usually made them in multiples of two, so that there was no middle projection that people could blithely adopt as the most probable. Sometimes there were as many as four or six, so that you had to read the assumptions to figure out which one you wanted to take. But I'm not sure that really worked.

Robert Engelman: Population projections take off from a point that is about fifteen to twenty years in the future. You know that unless there are dramatic changes in delaying childbirth and increasing the spacing of children, your population will grow by a predictable amount between now and twenty years from now. The amount of population growth is built in, because those who will make up the next generation of parents are already alive. They're likely to have at least two and probably three children, on the average. So we know about what the population will probably be over the next twenty years.

Nicholas Eberstadt: As a general matter, population projections, in the period for which they're accurate, aren't interesting; in the period where they get really interesting, they aren't accurate. The reason for this is that they're driven by fertility assumptions. Over a period of fifteen years you can get quite a change in fertility.

Robert Engelman: Rather than just trying to reduce the total fertility rate and discourage large families, you get a pretty big bang for the buck by working to *delay pregnancy* and *space pregnancies*. The fact that around the world today girls are having babies so young, and so close together, is a major factor in population growth. Perhaps this is an area where there ought to be common ground between the two sides of the population growth question. We share an interest in policies that allow women to wait a while, to refrain from having babies before they're married, and then to space out their pregnancies. This can have a dramatic impact on the population growth rate. Yet people can still have the number of children that they want.

3

How Population Growth Affects Human Progress

Julian Simon and Karl Zinsmeister

M any Americans believe that population growth inevitably slows
economic development, increases global poverty, reduces the
food supply, and degrades the environment. The reason for this widespread mistaken belief is not hard to find. For more than thirty years,
prominent international institutions have misanalyzed such world
development problems as hunger, illiteracy, pollution, resource exhaustion, and slow economic growth. The World Bank, the State
Department's Agency for International Development (AID), the
United Nations Fund for Population Activities (UNFPA), and the
environmental organizations have asserted that the cause of all these
problems is population growth.

Public worry was heightened in 1968 by Paul Ehrlich's best-selling
book describing population growth as a "bomb" that would "explode"
during the 1970s, causing hundreds of millions of deaths, leading to
war and violence, and jeopardizing the planet's ability to support life.

Julian Simon, who teaches business administration at the University of
Maryland, is the author of several books on population economics, including
Population Matters (1990) and *The Ultimate Resource* (1981). **Karl Zinsmeister**
is the editor of *The American Enterprise,* a bi-monthly magazine published by
the American Enterprise Institute.

61

Five years later the president of the World Bank, Robert McNamara, wrote:

> The greatest single obstacle to the economic and social advance-
> ment of the majority of the peoples in the underdeveloped world
> is rampant population growth. . . . The threat of unmanageable
> population pressures is very much like the threat of nuclear war. . . .
> Both threats can and will have catastrophic consequences unless
> they are dealt with rapidly. [*One Hundred Countries, Two Billion
> People* (London: Pall Mall Press, 1973), 45-46.]

Even children "know" that the natural environment is deteriorat-
ing, that food is in increasingly short supply, and that population size
and growth are the villains. A children's book called the *Golden Stamp
Book of Earth and Ecology* asserts, "All of the major environmental
problems can be traced to people—more specifically, to too many
people." But these supposed facts that are taught to children with so
much assurance are either unproven or wrong. For a quarter of a
century now, a solid body of statistical evidence has contradicted the
conventional wisdom about the effects of population growth in less
developed countries. Research by economists has shown that much
of the alleged economic harm from population growth has not occurred. And studies by social historians indicate that population
growth is often used as a scapegoat for problems with other causes,
especially a lack of economic and political freedom.

The error in public understanding of population growth has cost
us all dearly by directing our attention away from the factor that we
now know is central to a country's economic development: its
economic and political system. Furthermore, misplaced belief that
population growth slows economic development has been the basis
for inhumane programs of coercion and the denial of personal liberty
in one of the most valued choices a woman and man can make: the
number of children they wish to bear and raise.

At first glance, the demographic facts are indeed frightening. The
human population appears to be expanding at an exponential rate,
restrained only by starvation and disease. It seems that without some
drastic intervention to check this geometric growth there will soon be
"standing room only."

Worry about population growth is not new. Euripides, Polybius,

Plato, and Tertullian are on record as citizens who feared that population growth would cause food shortages and environmental degradation. In the late eighteenth century, the British economist Thomas Malthus did "standing room only" arithmetic apparently proving that population growth would inevitably outstrip expanding resources and bring death and disaster. In 1802, a Dutch colonial official wrote that Java, with a population of 4 million, was "overcrowded with unemployed." Now a third of Indonesia's nearly 180 million people live in Java, and again the island is said to be overcrowded.

The Ebb and Flow of Population Growth

The common view of population growth—especially as it occurs in poor countries—is that people breed "naturally." Poor people are assumed to have sexual intercourse without concern for the possible consequences. In the words of the environmentalist William Vogt, whose book *Road to Survival* (1948) sold millions of copies, population growth in Asia is the result of "untrammeled copulation" by "the backward billion." A. J. Carlson, a physician, wrote in a 1955 issue of the *Journal* of the American Medical Association, "If we breed like rabbits, in the long run we have to live and die like rabbits." This idea goes hand in hand with the view that population growth will increase geometrically until starvation or disease halts it.

The idea of "natural breeding," "natural fertility," or "untrammeled copulation" has been buttressed by experiments in animal ecology, which some biologists say can serve as models of human population growth. The analogies that have been proposed include John B. Calhoun's famous observations of Norwegian rats in a pen, the putative behavior of flies in a bottle or of germs in a bucket, and the proclivities of meadow mice and cotton rats—creatures that keep multiplying until they die for lack of sustenance. But as Malthus himself acknowledged in the revised edition of his *Essay on the Principle of Population*, human beings are very different from flies or rats. When faced with a bottle-like situation, people are capable of foresight and may abstain from having children for "fear of misery." That is, people can choose a level of fertility to fit the resources that will be available. Malthus wrote, "Impelled to the increase of his species by an equally powerful instinct, reason interrupts his career, and asks him whether he may not bring beings into the world, for whom he cannot provide the means of support."

Demographic history offers evidence that people can also alter the limit. That is, they can increase resources when they need to. Population growth seems not to have been at all constant or steady over the long sweep of time. According to the paleo-ecologist Edward Deevey, the broadest picture of the past million years shows three momentous and sudden changes. The first such change, a rapid increase in population around 1 million B.C., followed the innovations of tool-using and tool-making. Deevey speculates that the various tools "gave the food gatherer and hunter access to the widest range of environments." But once the new power from the use of tools had been exploited, the rate of population growth fell and population size became almost stable.

The next rapid jump in population started perhaps 10,000 years ago, when men began to keep herds and to plow and plant the earth, rather than simply foraging for the plants and game that grew naturally. Once again, the rate of population growth abated after the initial productivity gains from the new technology had been exploited, and again population size became nearly stable in comparison with the previous rapid growth.

These two episodes of a sharp rise and a subsequent fall in the rate of population growth suggest that the present rapid growth—which began in the West between 250 and 350 years ago—may also slow down when, or if, the new industrial and agricultural knowledge that followed the Industrial Revolution begins to yield fewer innovations. Of course, the current knowledge revolution may continue without a foreseeable end. Either way, over the long term, population size can be seen to adjust to productive conditions, contrary to the popular belief in continual geometric growth. In this view, population growth represents economic success and human triumph, rather than failure.

Deevey's account of population history leaves us with the impression that population growth has an irresistible, self-reinforcing logic of its own. That perspective is so broad, however, that it can be misleading. For example, even in as large an area as Europe, where local ups and downs might be expected to cancel each other out, population from 14 A.D. to 1800 did not grow at a constant rate, nor did it always grow. Instead, there were advances and reverses, provoked by a variety of forces.

Population doesn't simply rise until it butts up against famine or epidemic or some other hard constraint. Reduction in fertility can be expected even if technical innovation and increasing productivity continue at their current high levels, because parents adjust to social and productive conditions.

For one thing, income has a decisive effect on population. Along with a temporary jump in fertility as income rises in poor countries comes a fall in child mortality, because of better nutrition, better sanitation, and better health care (in the twentieth century child mortality has declined in some poor countries without a rise in income). As people see that fewer births are necessary to achieve a given family size, they adjust fertility downward. Increased income also brings education and contraception within reach of more people, makes children more expensive to raise, and perhaps influences the desire to have children. It usually initiates a trend toward city living; in the city, children cost more and produce less income for the family than they do in the country.

At present, the birth rate is far below replacement level—that is, below zero population growth—for a number of the largest countries in Europe, such as Germany, Italy, and Spain. Fertility has been falling in the developing countries as well. As recently as 1970, the women of the less developed world (as defined by the World Bank) were bearing an average of 6 children each. By the end of the 1980s that average was down to about 3.5. When you consider that about 2.2 children would produce a steady-state population (that is, each generation merely replacing its parents, plus a small allowance for childhood mortality, childless adults, and the like), then this remarkable fact emerges: In just the last two decades, the less developed world has moved almost three-fifths of the way toward a fertility rate that would yield "zero population growth." So we can be quite sure that the European pattern of demographic transition is being repeated now in other parts of the world as mortality falls and income rises.

Forecasters' Fallibility

When we look at the demographic facts with an eye to judging what ought to be done about population, we want to know what the future holds, how great the "pressures" of population size and growth will be. However, the history of demographic predictions gives us reason to be humble about turning forecasts into policy. In the 1930s, most Western countries expected and feared a decline in their populations. The most extensive investigation of the matter was undertaken in Sweden, in 1935, by some of the world's best social scientists. All four of their projections predicted that the Swedish population would decline by as much as two million by 1985. But their hypotheses about the future—intended to bracket all conceivable possibilities—turned out to be wrong, for the population has instead *grown* by about two million. If the Swedes had introduced fertility-increasing programs, as the demographers advised, the results would have been contrary to what they now want.

The Swedes were not alone in making inaccurate, pessimistic forecasts. A research committee of eminent scientists appointed by Herbert Hoover in 1933 reported that "we shall probably attain a population between 145 and 150 million during the present century." None of a variety of forecasts made in the 1930s and 1940s by America's demographic experts predicted a population as large as 200 million people even for the year 2000, but the United States reached that level around 1969 and is far beyond it now. A good many of the forecasters actually predicted a decline in population before the year 2000.

There is no reason to believe that contemporary forecasting methods are better than older ones. In 1976, "the best demographic estimates" of world population for the year 2000 set it at "nearly 7 billion," according to Rafael Salas, executive director of the United Nations Fund for Population Activities (UNFPA). But by 1979, Salas was projecting nearly 6 billion people by 2000. In three years, his estimate had declined by almost a billion people, or nearly one-seventh.

In the United States, as recently as 1972, the President's Commission on Population Growth forecast that "even if the family size drops gradually—to the two-child average—there will be no year in the next two decades in which the absolute number of births will be less than in 1970." How did it turn out? In 1971—the year before this forecast was transmitted to the President and then published—the absolute number of births (not the birth rate) was already less than in 1970. By 1975, the absolute number of births was barely higher than in 1920, and the number of white births was actually lower than in most years between 1914 and 1924. In this case, the commission did not even backcast correctly, let alone forecast well. Mistakes like this ought to encourage a little skepticism about demographic predictions.

Making forecasts of population size requires making assumptions about people's choices, and such assumptions are sometimes wrong, as we have seen. We can expect that income will continue to rise, but how much of their income will people expect a child to cost? What other activities will compete with child-rearing for parents' interest and time? Such hard-to-predict choices are likely to be the main determinants of population growth. We can at least say confidently, however, that the growth of population during the past few centuries is no proof that population will continue to grow straight upward toward infinity and doom.

Population Growth and Economic Growth

The heart of all economic theory of population, from Malthus to the 1972 MIT researchers' study *The Limits to Growth,* can be stated in a single sentence: The more people using a stock of resources, the lower the income per person, if all else remains equal. This proposition derives from what economists have called the law of diminishing returns: Two men cannot use the same tool, or farm the same piece of land, without producing less than they would produce if they did not have to share. A related idea is that two people cannot nourish themselves as well from a given stock of food as one person can. The age distribution that results from a high birth rate reinforces this effect, for the number of children in proportion to workers is larger. Also, the more children women have, the less chance they have to work outside the home, so the proportionate size of the work force is diminished further.

According to this reasoning, both sheer numbers of people and the age distribution that occurs in the process of getting to the higher numbers ought to have the effect of a smaller per capita product. But the evidence does not confirm the conventional theory. It suggests that population growth almost certainly does not hinder, and perhaps even helps, economic growth.

One piece of historical evidence is the concurrent explosion of both population and economic development in Europe from 1650 onward. Further evidence comes from a comparison of the rates of population growth and output per capita in those developed countries for which data on the past century are available. No strong relationship between the two variables appears. For example, population has grown six times faster in the United States than in France, but the rate of increase in output per capita has been about the same. The populations of Great Britain and Norway grew at the same pace for the past century, but Norway's output per capita increased about a third faster. Australia, on the other hand, had a very fast rate of population growth, but its rate of increase in output per capita was quite slow.

Studies comparing rates of population growth with rates of economic growth are another source of evidence. They have shown that per capita income has been growing as fast or faster in less developed countries as in developed countries, despite the fact that population has grown faster in the less developed countries. These statistical studies of the relation between population growth and economic growth begin in the mid-sixties with an analysis by the Nobel-winning economist Simon Kuznets covering the few countries for which data are available over the past century, and analyses by Kuznets and Richard Easterlin of the data covering many countries since World War II. The studies agree that faster population growth is not associated with slower economic growth. Peter Bauer, perhaps the most influential economic-development theorist alive today, summarizes the statistical record by saying that rapid population growth "has not inhibited economic progress either in the West or in the contemporary Third World."

The relation between economics and fertility is the reverse of what population-explosionists argue: it is not that slower population growth brings prosperity, but rather that prosperity brings slower population growth. Fertility levels reflect a society's level of development and proceed apace with it. Small families are a symptom, not a cause, of socio-economic advancement. That is, as countries develop economically, fertility tends to fall. Costs and benefits of having children change with the shift from rural to urban living along with increases in education and shifts in attitudes. This is the famous "demographic transition."

Population Density and Economic Growth

The research-wise reader may wonder whether population *density* might be more important than population growth. But the data show that higher density is generally associated with better rather than poorer economic results. To see an example, visit Hong Kong, which just a few decades ago seemed to be without prospects because of insoluble resource problems. Marvel at its astonishing collection of modern highrise apartments and office buildings, and take a ride on its excellent, smooth-flowing highways. You will soon realize that a very dense concentration of human beings—well over forty times the density of China—does not prevent comfortable existence and exciting economic expansion, as long as the economic system gives individuals the freedom to exercise their talents and to take advantage of opportunities.

A visitor to Hong Kong in the 1950s saw huge masses of impoverished people without jobs—thousands of them sleeping every night on the sidewalks or on small boats—on an island with a total lack of exploitable natural resources. Returning just three decades later, the visitor saw bustling crowds of healthy people full of hope and energy. The experience of Singapore demonstrates that Hong Kong is not unique, for both Singapore's population density and its soaring per-person income are like Hong Kong's. Two examples do not prove the case, of course, but many other countries similarly show that population density does not veto progress in economics and quality of life. The rocky islands of Japan house a highly productive society whose 125 million people are among the richest and longest-lived in the world. Holland, which clearly supports its population very well, has a population density of 373 people per square kilometer—nearly 50 per cent higher than the density of India, which is considered by many to be overpopulated.

Other contrasting situations, too, show the folly of attributing wealth or poverty to the density of the population. The United States and Germany are among the richest nations in the world; the United States is sparsely populated, with 27 people per square kilometer, while Germany is densely populated—226 people per square kilometer. South Korea has 444 per square kilometer, yet its economy is one of the fastest growing on earth. A very slow-growing and poor nation is thinly populated Bolivia, with just 7 persons per square kilometer. The poorest nation on the globe, Ethiopia, is also one of the more sparsely populated—47 per square kilometer.

In brief, many lightly populated countries are poor and hungry, and many densely populated countries are prosperous and healthy. The point here is not that population density is an advantage (though the statistical analyses show that it is), but rather that it is not the critical variable in determining a society's prospects.

The 1986 NRC-NAS Report

Agreement with the viewpoint expressed here is growing. The "official" turning point came in 1986 with the publication of a report by the National Research Council and the National Academy of Sciences (NRC-NAS) entitled "Population Growth and Economic Development." This report almost completely reversed a 1971 report on the same subject from the same source. In regard to raw materials, which have been the subject of so much alarm, NRC-NAS concluded: "The scarcity of exhaustible resources is at most a minor constraint on economic growth. The concern about the impact of rapid population growth on resource exhaustion has often been exaggerated." The general conclusion goes only this far: "On balance, we reach the qualitative conclusion that slower population growth would be beneficial to economic development for most developing countries." That is, NRC-NAS found forces operating in both positive and negative directions. This is a major break with the monolithic characterizations of the past, in which additional people were always seen as a major drag upon development.

The NRC-NAS report emphasized that the crucial variable in determining whether a particular country flourishes or flounders is the structure of its economic and political institutions, not the number of people. The "key" factor, wrote the authors, is the "mediating role that human behavior and human institutions play in the relation between population growth and economic processes." They urged the importance of free markets in achieving development, suggesting that the path to both higher income and lower birth rates is freer economies.

As a hard-headed scientific document assembled by some of the world's most prominent experts on population and economic development, the NRC-NAS report caused a considerable stir in the demographic community. Allen Kelley described it as "a watershed. . . . It retreats very substantially from many previous assessments which concluded that population growth exerted a strong negative impact on development." Unfortunately, the study was poorly reported in the press and has had less effect on public opinion than it should have had.

The Resource-Creation Process

The layman inevitably wonders: How can the persuasive common sense embodied in the Malthusian theory be wrong? To be sure, in the short run an additional person—baby or immigrant—means a lower standard of living for everyone. Given a fixed available stock of goods, an increase in consumers means smaller portions for all. More workers laboring with a fixed available stock of capital means less output per worker.

But if the resources are not fixed, then the Malthusian logic of diminishing returns does not apply. And the plain fact is that, given some time to adjust to shortages, the resource base does not remain fixed. People create more resources of all kinds. When horse-powered transportation became insufficient to meet needs, the railroad and the motor car were developed. When schoolhouses become crowded, we build new schools—more modern and better than the old ones.

As with man-made resources, so it is with natural resources. Replacements are found. When a shortage of elephant tusks jeopardized the production of billiard balls in the last century, a prize was offered for a substitute for the ivory, and celluloid was invented. The rest of our plastics followed. When trees became scarce in the sixteenth century, the English learned to use coal in industry. Satellites and fiber-optics derived from sand replace now expensive copper for telephone transmission. Extraordinary as it seems, natural-resource scarcity—that is, the cost of raw materials, which is the relevant economic measure of scarcity—has tended to decrease rather than to increase over the entire sweep of history. This trend is at least as reliable as any other trend observed in human history. The prices of all natural resources, measured in the wages necessary to pay for given quantities of them, have been falling as far back as data exist. A pound of copper now costs an American only a twentieth of what it cost in hourly wages two centuries ago, and perhaps a thousandth of what it cost 3,000 years ago.

The most extraordinary part of the resource-creation process is that temporary or expected shortages, whether due to population growth, income growth, or other causes, tend to leave us better off than we would have been had the shortages never arisen. The new resources usually turn out to be cheaper than the old ones. Often they are better. And we reap a continuing benefit from the intellectual and physical capital created to meet the shortage.

Practically speaking, there are no resources until we find them, identify their possible uses, and develop ways to obtain and process them. We perform these tasks with increasing skill as technology develops. Hence scarcity diminishes.

Besides, the trend with modern economic development is that natural resources become less and less important. Extractive industries are only a very small part of a modern economy, say a twentieth or less, whereas they constitute the lion's share of poor economies. Japan and Hong Kong prosper despite their lack of natural resources; such independence was impossible in earlier centuries. And although agriculture is thought to be a very important part of the American economy, if all our agricultural land passed out of our ownership tomorrow, our loss of wealth would equal only about a ninth of one year's gross national product. We would buy agricultural products abroad at hardly higher prices.

From the standpoint of economic production, one crucial natural resource *is* becoming more scarce: human beings. Yes, there are many more people on earth now than there were a few decades ago. But if we measure the scarcity of people the same way we measure the scarcity of economic goods—by the market price—then people are indeed becoming more scarce, because the price of labor has been rising almost everywhere in the world.

No sooner is one fear about population growth scotched than another takes its place. The latest is the effect of population growth upon education: although a higher birth rate may not threaten natural-resource exhaustion, certainly it must imply less education per person. But once again, it just isn't so. Studies have shown that societies with a relatively high proportion of children somehow find the resources to educate their children as well or almost as well as do countries at similar income levels with lower birth rates. Outstanding examples of countries with high rates of education in the face of relatively large numbers of children include the Philippines, Costa Rica, Peru, Jordan, and Thailand.

How Population Growth Can Help the Economy

There are several ways in which population growth can encourage economic progress rather than economic decline:

■ People make special efforts when they perceive a special need. For example, for each additional child an American father works extra the equivalent of two to five weeks a year. In the long run, this yearly 4 to 10 percent increase in work may fully (or more than fully) balance the temporary loss of labor by the mother. (The other side of this coin is that people may slack off when population growth slows and demand lessens.)

■ The larger proportion of young people in the labor force that results from population growth has advantages. Young workers produce more in relation to what they consume than older workers, largely because the older workers receive increases in pay with seniority, regardless of productivity. And because each generation enters the labor force with more education than the previous generation, the average worker becomes more and more knowledgeable.

■ Population growth creates business opportunities and facilitates change. It makes expansion investment and new ventures more attractive by reducing risk and by increasing total demand. For example, if housing is over-built or excess capacity is created in an industry, a growing population can take up the slack and remedy the error.

■ More job opportunities and more young people working mean that there will be more mobility within the labor force. And mobility greatly enhances the efficient allocation of human resources: the best matching of people to jobs.

■ Population growth promotes "economies of scale." Often there is greater efficiency with larger-scale production. Through this mechanism, the more people, the larger the market, and therefore the greater the need for bigger and more efficient machinery, division of labor, and improved transportation and communication. It is an established economic truth that the faster an industry grows, the faster its efficiency improves. A study that compared the output of selected U.S. industries with the output of those same industries in the United Kingdom and Canada showed that if you quadruple the size of an industry, you may expect to double the output per worker and per unit of capital employed. This should hold true for the developed world in general. A larger population also provides economies of scale for many expensive social investments that would not be profitable otherwise—for example, railroads, irrigation systems, and ports. And public services, such as fire protection, can also be provided at lower cost per person when the population is larger.

Population Growth and Technological Innovation

All these factors have economic force, but the most important benefit that population growth confers on an economy is an increase in the stock of useful knowledge. Your mind matters economically at least as much as, and perhaps more than, your mouth or hands. In the long run, the contributions people make to knowledge are great enough to overcome all the costs of population growth. This is a strong statement, but the evidence for it seems strong as well.

The importance of improved technological knowledge emerged clearly in two well-known studies, one by Robert Solow in 1957 and the other by Edward Denison in 1962. Using different methods, both calculated the extent to which the growth of physical capital and of the labor force could account for economic growth in the United States. Denison made the same calculations for Europe also. Both found that even after capital and labor are allowed for, much of the economic growth cannot be explained by any factor other than improvement in technological knowledge and practice (including improved organization). From this point of view, the economies of scale attributable to larger factories do not appear to be very important, though technology improves more rapidly in large, fast-growing ones. This improvement in productivity isn't free; much of it is bought with investments in research and development. But that does not alter its importance.

What is the connection between innovation and population size and growth? Since ideas come from people, it seems reasonable that the number of improvements depends on the number of people using their heads. This is not a new idea. William Petty wrote in 1683 that "it is more likely that one ingenious curious man may rather be found out amongst 4 millions than 400 persons." Hans Bethe, who won the Nobel Prize for physics in 1967, has said that the prospects for nuclear fusion would be rosier if the population of scientists were larger.

"Money is not the limiting factor," he said. "Progress is limited rather by the availability of highly trained workers."

Even a casual consideration of history shows that as population has grown in the last century, there have been many more discoveries and a faster rate of growth in productivity than in previous centuries. In prehistoric times, progress was agonizingly slow. For example, whereas we routinely develop new materials—say, plastics and metals—millennia passed between the invention of copper metallurgy and the invention of iron metallurgy. If population had been larger, technological discoveries would surely have come along faster. Ancient Greece and Rome have often been suggested as examples contrary to this line of reasoning. But plotting the numbers of great discoveries, as recorded by historians of science who have made such lists, against Greek and Roman populations in various centuries shows that an increase in population or its rate of growth (or both) was associated with an increase in scientific activity, and population decline with a decrease.

In modern times, there is some fairly strong evidence to confirm the positive effect of population growth on science and technology. In countries at the same level of income, scientific output is proportional to population size. For example, the standard of living in the United States and in Sweden is roughly the same, but the United States is much larger than Sweden and it produces much more scientific knowledge. A comparison of the references used in Swedish and U.S. scientific papers and of the number of patented processes that Sweden licenses from the United States bears this out.

Well then, why isn't populous India a prosperous and advanced country? We have not argued that a large population will by itself overcome all the other variables in a society—its climate, culture, history, political structure. We have said only that there is no evidence that a large population creates poverty and underdevelopment. India is poor and underdeveloped for many reasons, and it might be even more so if it had a smaller population. The proper comparison is not between India and the United States but between India and other poor countries. India has one of the largest scientific establishments in the Third World, perhaps in part because of its large population.

It cannot be emphasized too strongly that "technological and scientific advance" does not mean only sophisticated research, and geniuses are not the only source of knowledge. Much technological advance comes from people who are neither well educated nor well paid: the dispatcher who develops a slightly better way of deploying the taxis in his ten-taxi fleet, the shipper who discovers that garbage cans make excellent cheap containers, the store manager who finds a way to display more merchandise in a given space, the stock clerk who finds a quicker way to stamp prices on cans, and so on.

Population growth spurs the adoption of existing technology as well as the invention of new technology. This has been well documented in agriculture, where, as population density increases, people turn to successively more "advanced" but more laborious methods of getting food—methods that may have been known but were ignored because they weren't needed. For example, hunting and gathering, which require very few hours of work a week to provide a full diet, give way to migratory slash-and-burn agriculture, which in turn yields to settled, long-fallow agriculture, which yields to short-fallow agriculture. Eventually fertilizing, irrigation, and multiple-cropping are adopted. Although each stage initially requires more labor than the one before, the end is a more efficient and productive system.

This phenomenon also explains why the advance of civilization is not a race between technology and population, each progressing independently of the other. Contrary to the Malthusian view, there is no direct link between each food-increasing invention and increased production of food. Some inventions, such as a better calendar for planting, may be adopted as soon as they prove successful, because they will increase production with no more labor. Others, such as settled agriculture or irrigated multi-cropping, require more labor, and thus will not be adopted until there is demand.

The fact that people learn by doing is a key to the improvement of productivity in particular industries, and in the economies of nations. The idea is simple: the bigger the population, the more of everything that is produced. With a greater volume come more chances for people to improve their skills and to devise better methods. Industrial engineers have understood this process for many decades, but economists first grasped its importance when they examined the production of airplanes during World War II. They discovered that when twice as many airplanes are produced, the labor required per plane is reduced by 20 percent. That is, if the first airplane requires 1,000 units of labor, the second will require 800 units, and so on, though after some time the gains from increased efficiency level off. Similar "progress ratios" describe the production of lathes, machine tools, textile machines, and ships. The effect of learning by doing can also be seen in the progressive reduction in price of new consumer products in the years following their introduction to the market—room air-conditioners and color television sets, for example.

Economic Growth: Comparing Countries

The international development institutions long considered it poor form to mention economic and political systems when they were discussing economic development. Compare China with Singapore. China's coercive population policy, including forced abortions, is often called "pragmatic" because its economic development supposedly requires population control. But Singapore, despite its very high population density, now suffers from a labor shortage, and it imports workers. It is even considering incentives for middle-class families to have more children, in contrast to its previous across-the-board anti-child-bearing policy. Defenders of China's policy say that Hong Kong and Singapore are different from China because they are city-states. But does that mean that if large hinterlands were attached to those "city-states" they would then become as poor as China?

Consider some pairs of countries that have the same culture and history and had much the same standard of living until they split apart after World War II: North Korea and South Korea; East Germany and West Germany; mainland China and Taiwan. The countries in each pair also started with much the same birth rates and population growth rates, but the centrally planned Communist countries had fewer people per square mile than the market-directed non-Communist countries.

The data clearly show—and even those who were ideologically predisposed not to accept the point now accept it—that the market-directed economies have performed much better economically, on every index of economic progress. Income per person is higher. Wages have grown faster. Indexes such as telephones per person are at a much higher level. Indicators of individual wealth and personal consumption, such as the number of autos and the amount of newsprint, show enormous advantages for the market-directed enterprise economies compared to the centrally planned, centrally controlled economies. Also, birth rates fell at least as fast in the market-directed countries as in the centrally planned countries.

These data provide solid evidence that an enterprise system works better economically than a planned economy. Furthermore, population growth poses less of a problem in the short run, and brings many more benefits in the long run, under conditions of freedom than in a government-controlled economy. China's problem is not too many people but rather a defective political-economic system. China might soon experience the same sort of labor shortage as Singapore, which is vastly more densely populated and has no natural resources, if it had free markets. (This does not mean a "free" system such as China has talked about in recent years; it is unlikely that a truly free market can coexist with a totalitarian political system, because a free economy is too great a political threat.)

Even the most skilled persons require a social and economic framework that rewards hard work and risk-taking, enabling their talents to flower. The key elements of such a framework are economic liberty, respect for property, fair and sensible rules of the market that are enforced equally for all, and the personal freedom that is particularly compatible with economic freedom.

What Should We Do About Population?

Should we encourage and aid countries to implement coercive population policies, as we have done in the past in China, India, Indonesia, and many other places? Those who answer affirmatively should be aware that the scientific evidence about the long-run economic consequences offers no support for such policies. And coercive policies interfere with personal liberty in one of the most precious choices a woman and man can make: the number of children they wish to bear and raise.

In the nineteenth century the planet Earth could sustain only one billion people. Now, five billion people are living longer and more healthily than ever before. The increase in the world's population represents our victory over death. Shouldn't we celebrate our new-found capacity to support human life—healthily, and with fast-increasing access to education and opportunity all over the world? It seems reasonable to expect that the energetic efforts of humankind will prevail in the future, as they have in the past, to increase worldwide our numbers, our health, our wealth, and our opportunities.

This is a message of receding limits and increasing resources and possibilities. It is a message of wealth creation, consistent with the belief that persons and firms, acting in search of their individual welfare and regulated only by the rules of a fair game, will produce enough to maintain and increase economic progress and promote liberty.

The doomsayers of the population-control movement preach a message of limits and decreasing resources, of a zero-sum game where one person gains wealth only at the expense of another, of fear and conflict and worry. They call for more governmental intervention in economics and in family affairs. Should we heed this message?

In the short run, all resources are limited, including the pulpwood that went into making this paper, the number of pages the editors will allow us to fill, and the attention the reader will devote to what we say. The longer run, however, is a different story. The standard of living has risen along with the size of the world's population since the beginning of recorded time. There is no convincing economic reason why this trend toward a better life should not continue indefinitely. Adding more people causes problems, but people are also the means to solve these problems. The main fuel of the world's progress is our stock of knowledge, and the brake is our lack of imagination. The ultimate resource is people, skilled, spirited, and hopeful people who will exert their wills and imaginations for their own benefit and, inevitably, for the benefit of us all.

A Further Word on
the New, Calmer Thinking

Karl Zinsmeister

I n recent years there has been some retreat from population alarmism, and three factors are behind the shift. One is the influence of
new statistical data on population growth and its effects, data that have
directly contradicted the claims and predictions of "population bomb"
theorists. A second factor is reaction against the gross human-rights
abuses committed in the 1970s and 1980s in the name of population
control. A third is important new theoretical research recently carried
out by a group of talented and iconoclastic scholars. The new, calmer
view of population growth may not be well reflected in popular and
mass-media discussions, but it has brought major changes in the
academic argument, in U.S. policy, and in U.N. programs. So let us
consider the three causative factors in more detail.

The New Data

The dire predictions of the population explosionists utterly failed to
come true. There were no population wars in the 1970s or 1980s. There
were no mass die-offs. There were famines, but they were not population famines. The loudly predicted calamities just didn't take place. And
indeed there were many pleasant surprises. For instance, Paul Ehrlich
wrote in *The Population Bomb* in 1968 that it was a "fantasy" to think that
India, which he cited as a paradigm of overpopulation, could feed itself
any time in the near future, "if ever." A participant in the Second
International Conference on the War on Hunger (also 1968) argued that
"the trend of India's annual grain production over the past eighteen

---

Karl Zinsmeister is the editor of *The American Enterprise*.

years leads me to the conclusion that the present output of about 95 million tons is a maximum level." The prevailing wisdom then was that we had entered a new area of limits, we had reached the end of the line economically in terms of advancing the quality of life, and we were going to have to learn to live with less.

Well, India's annual grain production now totals, not 95 million tons as in 1968, but over 150 million tons, and India is now actually a net exporter of food. The fact that even a country that used to be referred to as a basket case could produce this sort of a gain suggests that those who argue that food production can never keep up with population growth fail to appreciate how quickly new technology and improved economic practices (in this case Green Revolution agricultural products and new market incentives for farmers) can convert formerly redundant people into useful producers.

Another fact that the traditional population theorists did not fully appreciate was how fast the world was changing demographically. As mentioned earlier in this chapter, between 1970 and 1990, the average number of children borne by women in the less developed world declined from 6 to about 3.5. This is a tremendous drop, and I think it's fair to say that it took most demographers by surprise. In just two decades, the birth rate declined about three-fifths of the way toward 2.2, or "zero population growth." The problem of high fertility now seems to be in the process of solving itself in most places.

Still another fundamental fact often overlooked by population alarmists is that, contrary to popular claims, life quality in most of the Third World has been rapidly *improving,* not declining, during the last few decades. Those were, of course, the very decades when population was growing the fastest. Over the last thirty years, the Third World infant-mortality rate has been almost cut in half. Life expectancy at birth has risen by about twenty years. Adult literacy rates in the less developed world have more than doubled since 1960. The claim that rapid population growth vetoes social progress and economic progress runs head on into some very strong countervailing evidence.

Reaction Against Abuses

The second factor that has produced some skepticism about the international population-control movement is its record of human-rights violations over the last two decades. In 1976 the Indian government declared, "Where a state legislature . . . decides that the time is ripe and it is necessary to pass legislation for compulsory sterilization, it may do so." In the six months following that ruling, more than six million Indians were sterilized, many thousands forcibly so. That episode inspired such fierce grassroots resistance that the government of Indira Gandhi was eventually brought down.

Even before the government issued its public justification, coercion in the name of population control had been rife in India. The distinguished American demographer Richard Easterlin reports that when he was a member of a United Nations Family Planning Mission to India in 1969, program administrators in Bombay told him how strong-arm tactics were used in the slum districts to ensure that government vasectomy targets were met. When Easterlin expressed concern at this, the surprised official answered that "surely the end justifies the means." And high international officials supported these injustices. In November 1976, after the forced sterilization program had been unveiled, World Bank president Robert McNamara paid a personal visit to the Indian family-planning minister to "congratulate him for the Indian Government's political will and determination in popularizing family planning."

An even more extensive campaign of intimidation and violence in the name of population control has been and continues to be conducted in China. In the early 1980s reports began to reach the West —through, for instance, the work of Stanford anthropologist Stephen Mosher—that the Chinese government was exerting enormous and often brutal pressure on couples to limit their family size to one child. What made this accumulating evidence unignorable in official Washington was a graphic series of three articles in the *Washington Post* in January 1985. After returning from a four-year assignment in China, *Post* reporter Michael Weisskopf was finally free to publish his findings about population-control practices without risking expulsion from the country. I will quote at some length from his report:

China's family-planning work is backed by the full organizational might of the Communist Party, which extends its influence to every factory, neighborhood, and village. Every Chinese belongs to a . . . workplace or rural governing [unit], and every unit has a birth control committee headed by party officials. These officials . . . carefully plan new births for their unit, requiring written applications from any couple wanting to have a child, and matching requests with quotas that trickle down from Peking.

[One campaign in northern China], described by a participating doctor, began in November 1983, when officials from every commune in the county searched their records for women under the age of 45 with two or more children. Then they broadcast their names over public loudspeakers and set dates by which each had to report to the clinic for [sterilization]. There was a warning to potential evaders: the loss of half of their state land allotment, a fine of $200— equal to about a year's income—and a late fee of $10 for every day they failed to report. . . . [Such a campaign often sends] whole villages of eligible women into hiding. To head off a mass exodus last year in coastal Fujian province, officials reportedly organized late-night surprise attacks, hustling sleeping women from their beds to twenty-four-hour sterilization clinics. . . .

[Women are] required by national regulation to have IUDs inserted after their first child is born and are strictly forbidden to remove the stainless steel loops. . . . In some city hospitals, doctors automatically implant the devices immediately after a woman gives birth, often without informing the woman or seeking prior consent, according to a Peking gynecologist. . . .

Up to six times a year . . . [Chinese women] are stood before decades-old equipment to endure the kind of fluoroscopic examination discouraged in the West for fear of causing radiation damage to ovaries or fetuses. Frequent X-ray exams are considered necessary because of the high failure rate of IUDs, which are often inserted in a factory-line fashion without concern for sizing. . . . Few unauthorized pregnancies can elude the tight supervision of birth control activists, a phalanx of female members of the party . . . who are deputized by local officials to monitor the reproductive lives of Chinese couples. . . . They know everyone's contraceptive method and make daily house calls to remind birth control pill users to use their pills. . . . The activists closely watch for signs of pregnancy—morning sickness, craving for sour food, or swollen breasts—and cultivate informers to report on their neighbors or co-workers. They keep detailed records of every woman's menstrual cycle, checking to make sure of regularity. . . . [In some cases they post them, very often in workplaces so that if a woman is late everyone knows about it and can begin to exert pressure.]

First come the tactics of persuasion. . . . Several activists visit the pregnant woman's home to explain the need for population control. She is urged to have an abortion for the good of her nation, her community, her family. . . . If she holds her ground, the talks intensify. [Heavy fines and loss of state benefits are threatened.] The meetings go on, often all the way up to the point of delivery. Where talking fails, force often prevails. Sometimes officials use collective coercion in operations like that in Dongguan, where thousands of pregnant women were picked up in trucks and Jeeps, taken to commune headquarters for lectures, then driven to abortion clinics, some reportedly under police escort. [Michael Weisskopf, "Abortion Policy Tears Fabric of China's Society," *Washington Post,* January 7, 1985.]

This coercive family planning extends even to Chinese nationals living overseas. We know of Chinese couples studying in the United States in the late 1980s, for instance, who got letters from government officials back home ordering them to have an abortion when the wife got pregnant. They were told that if they did not do so, the entire factory or village from which they had come would be harshly punished.

The Indian and Chinese programs are the leading examples of human-rights abuses that have occurred in a number of different countries in the name of population control. And, scandalously, family planners and leaders of the population-control movement in the West have defended and rationalized harsh measures of these sorts. In 1983 the United Nations awarded its first U.N. medal for family-planning achievement. The joint winners were—you guessed it—the directors of the Indian and Chinese programs. The Chinese minister, a man named Qian Zin-Chong, explained a few months later that "the size of a family is too important to be left to the personal decision of a couple. Births are a matter of state planning."

Again, the sad fact is that it isn't merely officials of totalitarian nations that are willing to see this delicate family decision made by government fiat. In 1978, more than half of the members of the Population Association of America, which is this country's professional association for demographers, endorsed the opinion that "if world population continues to grow at its present rate, coercive birth control will have to be initiated." Fully a third of these professionals wanted some coercive birth control to begin immediately.

In the mid to late 1980s a number of prominent Western demographers developed arguments in favor of "beyond voluntary family planning" measures. A major 1984 World Bank report asserted that "ensuring that people have only as many children as they want . . . might not be enough." A 1986 study by leading U.S. academicians favorably entertained the idea of financial and legal penalties to manipulate a couple's childbearing decisions. In other words, important parts of the official international family-planning apparatus have begun to veer toward something much stronger than voluntary family planning. As John Aird wrote in his authoritative 1990 book, *Slaughter of the Innocents,* "The international family planning movement has crossed the line from humanitarianism into zealotry. It needs desperately to be called back before it does itself further damage." Richard Easterlin, one of the most honored deans of demography, has written,

> We have had sufficient experience now with population programs to realize that they can easily become a vehicle for elite pressure on the poor. I fear that the elevation to legitimacy of "beyond voluntary family planning" measures lends itself to precisely such pressure. . . . Of course one might claim that such measures are in the "ultimate" interest of the poor, but this view leaves one in the uncomfortable position of having to define the person, group, or institution that is better able to judge the interests of the poor than the poor themselves. [*"World Development Report 1984* Review Symposium," *Population and Development Review,* 1985, 119.]

Beyond this obvious potential for abuse of power, there is a deeper philosophical issue in this debate. The argument is sometimes made that the lives of certain Asian or African or Latin American peasants are miserable, and that "we who understand" cannot allow them to perpetuate their misery. But there is another point of view, which starts with the fundamental belief that there is dignity and potential in every human life and that even extraordinarily simple lives, even an existence that is deprived by modern standards, nonetheless can carry great meaning and pleasure. Those of us on the opposite side of the fence from the alarmists believe it is very dangerous to construct a generalized, systematic argument whose bottom line is that human beings are economic, social, and ecological nuisances—that, in short, people are a kind of pollution. That is a road to perilous territory.

The New Research

The third factor behind the calmer thinking on population is the new theoretical and empirical research on the *actual* results of population growth. Over the last decade, the prevailing arguments about the economic and social ill effects of population growth have been examined, one by one, and most have been found wanting. These arguments—about resource shortages, capital dilution, unemployment and schooling problems, and the like—were taken up earlier in this chapter. Suffice it to say here that the predictions of the population-bombers haven't proven out very impressively.

One of the insights of the new demographic thinking is that the number of people a given area can "support" is subject to constant change, and is related to how the people are organized economically and socially. There are 125 million people jammed onto the rocky islands of Japan. Yet, because of their well-structured and highly productive social system, they are among the richest and longest living people in the world.

The table of "Population Densities" on page 87 makes it apparent that there is no predictable relationship between population density and economic success. The number of people is not the critical variable in determining a society's success. In most places where there is squalor, hunger, and high unemployment, the problem is not *overpopulation* but *underproduction*. People do not only consume, they also produce—food, capital, even resources. More precisely, they produce the ideas that transform a useless resource—say, bauxite sixty years ago—into a useful resource.

The vital requirement for every nation and its leaders is to organize the society economically and politically so that each person will be an asset rather than a burden. In a country whose economy is a mess, each additional baby can be an economic problem; but if the country is structured in such a way as to allow that child to labor and think creatively, he becomes an asset.

What prevents almost all developing countries from providing for their growing populations is not a lack of family-planning programs, nor a shortage of natural resources, nor a lack of Western aid. Rather, it is a *defective economy and government.* Those concerned for the welfare of people in poor countries around the globe ought to focus, not on

Population Densities of Rich and Poor Nations in 1992

	People per sq. km	Per capita GNP
Japan	329	$28,190
United States	27	23,240
Germany	226	23,030
Netherlands	373	20,480
Hong Kong	5,536	15,360 (GDP)
South Korea	444	6,790
Brazil	18	2,770
Guatemala	91	980
Bolivia	7	680
China	124	470
Nigeria	113	320
India	272	310
Bangladesh	794	220
Ethiopia	47	110

Source: World Development Report 1994, The World Bank

raw numbers, but on the institutions that prevent citizens from exercising their creative and productive potential.

A Response

Rodolfo A. Bulatao

Julian Simon and Karl Zinsmeister make an interesting and occasionally even elegant argument that fewer babies is not the key to improving human welfare. I wonder, however, with whom they are having the argument. They seem to be arguing with some dead philosophers and economists, some living ecologists, perhaps some shadowy demographers. But they are *not* having the argument with the men and women in developing countries who are producing the babies. These men and women, by the millions and the hundreds of millions, are today choosing to have fewer children.

Here are the facts. In 1990 in Africa, over 20 million couples were using contraception. In Latin America and the Caribbean the figure was over 40 million; in Asia, over 300 million. Total in the developing world in 1990: about 365 million couples—just about half of all married couples in developing countries. The total is also, incidentally, almost three times the number of couples in industrial countries who use contraception.

In addition, large numbers of couples in developing countries want to avoid childbearing, either in the immediate future or indefinitely, but are not now doing anything to prevent it. These are the people who are characterized by demographers as having an "unmet need" for contraception. In this group, generally, are at least 10 percent of reproductive-age women in each developing country that has been surveyed, and as many as 40 percent in a few countries. The total unmet need is so large that, in practically all developing countries outside sub-Saharan Africa, filling the need would bring fertility down essentially to replacement level.

Rodolfo A. Bulatao is a senior demographer with the Population and Human Resources Department of the World Bank, Washington, D.C.

Some of the most dramatic evidence about what this unmet need means comes from Kenya. In 1989, unmet need was estimated from a Demographic and Health Survey at a sky-high 40 percent of married women, perhaps the highest percentage in the world. Another survey was done in 1993. In the earlier survey, total fertility—that is, the number of children a woman would have if she followed the experience of the different cohorts in the survey—was estimated at 6.7. In the new survey it is 5.4. This 20 percent decline in just four years is one of the most rapid ever recorded. A lot of it has to do, undoubtedly, with the huge previously unmet need.

Now, Simon and Zinsmeister are not entirely innocent about this huge need for contraception. In fact, they argue that it is a natural process: "Population size [they say] can be seen to adjust to productive conditions." Given the historically unprecedented declines in death rates that have taken place over the last half century, a similarly rapid fertility decline would seem to be an inevitable and appropriate adjustment.

We come now to the real issue: what we think about this adjustment; what we think about all these men and women who either use contraception or would prefer to avoid childbearing even though they have not yet brought themselves to the contraceptive option, or have not had it available. Do we approve of their choice? Do we facilitate their acting on it? Or do we oppose it and try to convince them to produce the babies instead?

Simon and Zinsmeister give this answer: "The number of children that [a woman and man] wish to bear and raise" is "one of the most valued choices [they] can make." With this I totally agree. Women and men should be provided with all the information they need to make such a valued choice responsibly and should be assisted as much as practicable in implementing it. That is what voluntary family-planning programs—practically all family-planning programs in the developing world—attempt to do. They provide people with choices and the ability to implement them.

Why should people need help in implementing their choices? Well, contraception is often not a cheap choice. The retail price for an annual supply of contraceptive pills, or an annual supply of condoms, exceeds a hundred dollars in half a dozen developing countries. In many developing countries, it takes 5 percent or more of average annual income to pay the retail price for contraception—and possibly much more than 5 percent with incomes that are below average. Then there are the costs of ignorance, of simple unawareness of the options, of fear of what people will say, of the coercion that social norms can enforce.

Well, you might say, the World Bank commonly argues that governments should live within their means, adjust their spending downward, and make hard choices. Shouldn't families and households do the same? But that argument is a little strange. If people cannot afford contraception, should they then be forced to have children, after which they will be even less able to afford other necessities?

When governments abdicate their responsibilities, the results can be reproductive health disasters. In Brazil, the government looked the other way and allowed pharmacies to provide most contraceptive pills without counseling, almost guaranteeing a high failure rate. This has led to nearly as many abortions as live births, so that septic abortions and misuse of abortion-inducing chemicals are a major women's health problem. The only alternative for many Brazilian women has been sterilization, obtained by submitting to a Caesarean section and making a side payment to the attending physician. If the government had stepped in earlier, much pain and suffering, and many deaths, could have been avoided.

Will it be good for their welfare if people's choices involve substantial use of contraception? We almost don't have to ask that question. If it is their choice, and they are in full command of the facts, I don't think we have any reason to second-guess them. The evidence is quite clear that avoidance of certain births would improve infant and maternal health. Certain births carry very high risks: births to very young women, births that are too close together, births to women who already have several children. For example, in Egypt, if a woman has two births within eighteen months, the risk of a child death is triple what it would be if the babies were further apart. In Jamaica, the risk with a fourth birth is 65 percent higher than the risk with a third birth. So at least from the point of view of health, there is little question that contraception is good for women and children.

Should we worry that, if enough people adopt contraception, many of the least developed countries will never attain the population densities of the "Asian tigers," and therefore will never take off economically as these countries did? No, we should not. The populations of the Asian tigers are no longer growing as rapidly as they were, and the slowdown seems to have contributed to their economic growth.

We should not exaggerate the importance of demography for economic growth. Simon and Zinsmeister are correct in criticizing extreme views about the need for reducing rates of population growth. But they probably go too far in the other direction in claiming that rapid population growth must be a good thing. A book published for the World Bank in 1993 entitled *The East Asian Miracle* attempts to analyze what made these East Asian economies so successful. Seven fundamentals of their success are listed:

- a stable macroeconomy,
- a focus on early education in accumulating human capital,
- some attention to agriculture,
- use of banks to build a sound financial system,
- openness to foreign ideas and technology,
- allowing relative prices to reflect economic scarcities, and
- a successful export push.

Demography is not in this list but has a contributing role. The book argues that one of the fundamentals, the accumulation of human capital, was in fact considerably facilitated by properly timed reductions in human fertility. So fertility is a factor, a negative one tending to retard certain essential investments. And the book notes further that other countries that still have high rates of population growth find themselves on a treadmill with respect to poverty alleviation and human development efforts.

What I have argued, then, is this: (1) that hundreds of millions have chosen to limit their fertility, and hundreds of millions more are motivated to do so but need assistance; (2) that, to promote their welfare, it makes sense to provide them with assistance. The specific modalities of assistance—who should do it, whether the United States should be involved, how it should be done—are questions for another time.

Comments

Herb Schlossberg: I would like Julian Simon and Karl Zinsmeister to comment on something that isn't really covered in their paper: the question of culture—issues of motivation, of religious perspective, of views of reality, and so on. You deal with some of the ideas of P. T. Bauer but not with this idea of culture, which is something he raises from time to time.

Julian Simon: My view of culture comes from the sociologist Ron Friedman, one of the earliest and most influential thinkers in family planning. Friedman drew a diagram about twenty-five years ago with economic conditions on the left side, behavior on the right side, and values in between:

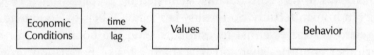

Yes, values and culture affect behavior, but only for a while, because they themselves are very much under the influence of underlying conditions.

Some examples of how Friedman's model is right: Roman Catholic families in poor Polish villages some fifty years ago had seven, eight, sometimes nine children, and everybody said, well, that's the Catholic culture. Then those families moved to the United States, and in no time they were having only two children. In Jewish families in North Africa, the mother would have seven or eight children, the older daughter might have six, and when they moved to Israel the younger daughter had two. Culture can affect behavior somewhat, but it seems

---

Note: Participants in this section are identified on pages 161-62.

to have relatively little continuing power. You see how culture is influenced by economic conditions with Chinese people in Hong Kong and a hundred miles north, in China. An American engineer in Hong Kong told me about the big difference in work behavior on construction sites where he worked in mainland China and in Hong Kong. Same people, originally; same language, same history, and so on. They work like hell privately in Hong Kong and they loaf on the government job in China, not because the culture is different but because the economic conditions are different.

Culture may be important, but I think it should be our last resort as an explanation. It's too easy to fall back on it and save ourselves the trouble of finding more objective explanations of behavior.

Karl Zinsmeister: I think I have found a small crack of disagreement between Julian and me. I certainly agree with him that sometimes things that are attributed to culture actually have other roots. However, I'm emphatically not a materialist, and I believe that values and cultural ideas have a big influence. My example would be the Mormons, who have a higher economic prosperity than median Americans and also have close to twice the fertility. And culture changes with geographic moves. Those Polish families that moved to the United States did not bring their Polish culture with them. Economics is certainly a part of fertility decisions and other social behavior, but I think that values are extremely important, too.

This is where I agree with a good bit of the P. T. Bauer thesis. And this also is relevant to the idea about unmet needs that Randy Bulatao brought up. I have absolutely no objection to providing services to couples who wish to control fertility but simply don't have the means. I am skeptical, however, that there is a gigantic demand for contraception that is not being met. The World Fertility Survey showed that in most of the countries of Africa the average woman *wants* over six children. You could airdrop free contraceptives all over the continent, you could provide them in every single hut and household, and there would still be a very high rate of childbirth in those African countries. What is missing is the *desire* to have fewer children. Now, if you posit the desire to have fewer children as a good, which I do not—I have no preference either way, and I don't think it's wise for governments to have a preference—then the way to get it is to change the desire for six or more children. The way that this can be done is cultural: you Westernize, you change the attitudes toward women's status, you educate. That brings us to the emphasis that Julian and I place on economic structures and political structures. They are extremely important in producing fertility outcomes.

Sheldon Richman: I read almost regularly in environmental publications about women in the Third World who seem to want more children than they are having. These publications state that providing information at low cost or free contraceptive devices is not going to get the fertility rates down. To do this requires what they call incentives and disincentives, which I see as a euphemism for coercion, since it has to do with taxes and jobs and electricity in villages. Those methods are not as outrageous as forced abortion, but they involve state manipulation of economic services and other factors in a state-dominated economy, and that is coercion. Garrett Hardin and others contend that the only way we are going to get fertility rates down is through these methods, because culture and other influences are keeping women from understanding that they ought to be having fewer children.

Rodolfo (Randy) **Bulatao**: I disagree. I don't think we need incentives, and I'm not in favor of them. Such changes as increases in female education and female employment and decreases in mortality rates are much more effective in bringing the fertility rate down than all the incentives we try to engineer.

Nicholas Eberstadt: I found the back-and-forth between Karl and Julian, on the one hand, and Randy, on the other, rather unsatisfactory. It doesn't seem to me that the argument has really been joined. Karl and Julian's paper is about the economic consequences of population growth. Randy's comments were a very modest justification of interventions in population through family-planning programs. I've known Randy for a long time, and I know that the World Bank is a big organization with a lot of different views represented. But I'd like to ask him a question: Do you personally think that there are macro-economic justifications for population interventions through subsidies? Do you think that there are arguments, apart from your argument of market failure, for interventions in population, such as the need to educate people, or the advantages or costs of avoiding a birth, or the economic dangers of rapid population growth?

Rodolfo (Randy) **Bulatao**: The macroeconomic evidence of the relationship between population growth and economic growth presents a problem. Population growth has three components: more babies, fewer deaths, and more migrants. Economic growth reduces the number of deaths; therefore population grows faster. It increases the number of immigrants; therefore population grows faster. Consequently, looking only at population growth as a whole and comparing it to economic growth is insufficient. You really have to look at the relationship between fertility and economic growth. Now, there's a lot of macroeconomic modeling on this. I'm not an expert in that field. What I understand is that there is evidence on both sides. My own intuition from this evidence is that rapid population growth is not good for economic development. It is not necessarily a major negative factor, but it is not good. The way I try to rationalize the conflicting evidence is to observe that a baby does not make an economic contribution. It takes twelve or fifteen or twenty years for him to make such a contribution. Thus, in the short run, you can lower economic growth by increasing population. Once the child is grown up, you might have faster economic growth. There is some modeling that, in fact, supports this idea of a generational lag.

The Asian tigers started reducing fertility at just the right time to give them their economic boost. Korea is a prime example of this: if they hadn't brought their fertility down, they would have spent twice as much of their GNP as they actually did to educate their new cohorts. I think there is an economic case for reducing high fertility, but it is a complex one to make.

I would like to say something about the World Bank also. The Bank is not an independent entity; it is owned by its stockholders, in most of the countries of the world, and we have to work with these stockholders. When the Bank intakes a loan, it is not a Bank project but a country project. It is also very diverse. The Bank gives considerable autonomy to people working on particular countries, so you will find a great deal of variety across Bank projects. The Bank is quite willing to be the fall guy, to be blamed for doing unpopular things. That is why we're willing to advocate structural adjustments. We do this because we think it is right, because we think that these kinds of things are necessary for economic development and the relief of poverty in these countries.

Susan Bratton: First of all, concerning the reduction in Third World fertility to 3.5, which Simon and Zinsmeister present as something wonderful: it would be nice to know where it came from. Some of that reduction happened naturally, through economic development and the like. But I know that women's groups and Planned Parenthood and a lot of governments have been working very hard at this in the past couple of decades. I do not think we should be too facile about where that reduced number comes from.

Also, what about the "losers" on the economic scene that also have high population growth rates? Would you say that voluntary reduction of population growth would be a mistake for some of these rural economies that seem to be very famine prone?

Julian Simon: The decline in population growth could be seen as something to cheer about or something to lament. My point was simply that the world was changing, and changing a lot faster than most people ever anticipated.

About those you call "losers": When you use the word "voluntary" and then refer to countries, I don't understand whose will is at work here. Is it the will of the individual person, or is it the will of some boss who says, "We will 'voluntarily' get it done"? What's the decision in question here, and made by whom?

Susan Bratton: Better public health services for more rural women. I agree that there's no way you do that without education. You must have a communication bridge, and the content of that communication automatically influences the view of the other person who is being approached. You're talking about moving technology into cultures that are not producing it themselves.

Julian Simon: As much as you are, I am in favor of any programs that will give people better health. But what has that got to do with population growth? I'm for helping them to better health so that they can have better lives, period. Bringing population growth into the matter only obscures the issue. Let's talk about bringing people to better lives by bringing them better health, better food, better education, all those things that are goods in themselves, and stop talking about population growth.

Karl Zinsmeister: This, again, is our argument: Reducing fertility is not an appropriate goal for any government. Individual couples have to be trusted with this decision. There are lots of positive and non-controversial things that governments can do to help their citizens— like encouraging markets and education—that will also probably have important effects on fertility. But let's not make fertility reduction the main goal or justification of governmental actions.

Gilbert Meilaender: Concerning coercion: To offer incentives or inducements is not necessarily coercive. From my outsider's perspective, I don't see how you can have any very complicated policy if it doesn't offer some sort of incentives or inducements. If you think that this always constitutes coercion and means that people's responses to it aren't in some way voluntary or free actions, well, none of us is ever a free agent, in any sense at all. It seems to me that we ought to assume that governments are going to offer incentives and inducements of all sorts, and that doing so is not necessarily coercive and not necessarily bad.

Karl Zinsmeister: I agree, basically, but with one important exception: In a state-directed economy where most job assignments and economic goodies come from a central directorate, financial incentives can be harshly coercive. Subsidizing or influencing is not terrifying in a decentralized economy. However, in places like China and India, for instance, there are plenty of cases where somebody who didn't get a vasectomy as officially urged to prevent the birth of a second child didn't get his taxi cab license renewed, or his factory promotion. And in a poor country, that can be a life-and-death loss.

Gilbert Meilander: That could be called an unjust use of incentives, but it's still perhaps not best categorized as coercion.

Jean Guilfoyle: These incentive programs can be as simple as offering a sari as a gift for undergoing sterilization. For people who have no clothing on their backs, a sari can be a strong incentive. When a farmer has crops that have not flourished, the small payment he is offered if his wife is sterilized can mean the difference between dying and surviving.

Jo Kwong: Both population issues and environmentalism are used as covers for achieving broader societal goals. I agree completely that family size must be an individual choice. As soon as we back down on that we are opening doors for institutional goals. The ultimate contribution of Karl and Julian's paper is the focus on the individual. We're not given resources; we're given raw materials that are made into resources through human contribution.

Bishop McHugh: On the question whether the apocalyptic approach is dead: I had occasion to read the preparatory document regarding the Cairo Conference presented to the U.N. General Assembly. The same old mindset is evident in that document: population growth is such a tremendous problem that we have to pull all the stops to forestall further growth. Jane Fonda has been designated the public-relations person for the U.N. Population Fund. She gave a twenty-page paper, and all its footnotes were to Garrett Hardin, Paul Ehrlich, and Lester Brown. Ms. Fonda trotted out this outdated and often erroneous thinking, plus some very pointed anti-Catholicism. The National Academy of Sciences has put out a new paper on population that goes back to the Hardin-Ehrlich approach. A considerable amount of apocalyptic thinking still drifts among the intellectual elites in the United States. It has become the prevailing philosophy in the Clinton administration.

Calvin Beisner: Perhaps in certain scholarly circles the apocalyptic notion is seen as irrelevant, but I find a nearly monolithic assumption among well-read lay people, people who read newspapers and magazines frequently, that population growth is an unmitigated disaster and that it spells certain famine and poverty in the world to come. Yesterday's mail brought this letter from Paul Ehrlich and Zero Population Growth: "DEAR FRIEND: Before you answer the enclosed ballot, take a quick trip with me through time. Imagine your life, a few short years from now. You're living in a world where fuel, food, jobs, housing and health care are at a premium. Where natural resources are severely depleted, cities horribly polluted, uncomfortably crowded and plagued by crime." The letter goes on to say, of course, that overpopulation underlies all these problems. This is precisely the sort of thing Ehrlich was saying thirty years ago. We have to be careful, as people who are scholars, not to confuse the scholarly world with the real world.

Someone earlier asked, What about the losers, the countries where there is still extreme poverty, high infant mortality rates, and so on? There are very few countries around the world where trends have been downward, and those downward trends that we do see have generally been short-term. The longer-term trends have been upward. Take sub-Saharan Africa. In some countries there, infant mortality tends to run as high as 100 per 1,000. That sounds just dreadful to us. Yet for sub-Saharan Africa as a whole, infant mortality fell by 32 percent in twenty-five years, from 1965 to 1990. It took forty years for Massachusetts to make the same improvement in infant mortality, from the same figure to the same figure, at the turn of the century. Sub-Saharan Africa is improving in that category faster now than Massachusetts did. We need to keep a historical perspective.

Karl Zinsmeister: I agree with Calvin Beisner that the average person doesn't have an inkling of the anti-alarmist argument that we have been discussing. If anything, people may be even more worried about this issue than they were twenty years ago. But let's not forget that for about eight years the U.S. government did the right thing. That's no mean accomplishment of the revisionist scholarship. In the 1984 Mexico City conference, we had some very sensible rhetoric for a change. That was an accomplishment. If intellectual moderates and truth-tellers persevere, good things are possible.

Julian Simon: Certain ideas will always be with us. The opposition to free trade, for instance, will never die, because the opposing idea —protection—is too commonsensical. And I think that population alarm and other doomsaying will always be with us, no matter how much we know and what anyone says to the contrary. We have had doomsayers as far back as we can go. It is somehow deep in the human psyche, and it will always be so. The best we can do is damage-control.

John Aird: One of the reasons why opinion is so slow to change is the factor of conflict of interests. Once you get an enterprise going in which you are raising funds for a stated purpose, you are very reluctant to reexamine the presumptions under which you started the enterprise. After all, it's your bread and butter. People within the profession of demography who are aware that the population-crisis case is flawed may be less than enthusiastic about making that fact known to the public. Demography gets the spin-off from family-planning funds, and has become a very prosperous profession since the public became aware of the notion of a population crisis.

Why don't the Ehrlichs of this world learn from their own experience? Well, they do. They learn that the population crisis sells. They learn that there is no accountability in the business of doomsaying: if one doom falls flat, raise another. There is not much reward in proclaiming that the population issue is less urgent than we had thought. You don't get funds for research with that kind of argument.

Karl Zinsmeister: I want to return to a point I made earlier and say that I hope no one thinks that Julian and I are saying things are fine. Things are *not* fine. The question is, *why* are they not fine? We're saying there are lots of sad reasons, so don't use population as a scapegoat. Conditions in some of the African countries, for instance, where I've worked, are heartbreaking. I think there is criminally corrupt and incompetent leadership in both the political and economic sectors in most of those countries. Until that is changed, no population level, no aid amount, no earnest effort by compassionate observers is going to do more than just slow the bleeding a little bit.

As for the environment: The only way you get better environmental and ecological results is if you're rich enough to pay for them. A sound environment is important, but it's never going to be at the top of the priority list. If you're hungry and your children are sick, then you're not going to worry about the environment. Only when those problems are under control will you begin to notice the smokestacks. Rational economic markets not only make people richer, they also make it possible for their societies to improve the quality of the water supply, to build sewage treatment plants, and so on. Anyone who is really interested in making the world less polluted should be very interested in market economics.

4

Population: Delusion and Reality

Amartya Sen

Few issues today are as divisive as what is called the "world population problem." During the months leading up to the 1994 International Conference on Population and Development, organized
by the United Nations and held in Cairo, these divisions among
experts received enormous attention and generated considerable heat.
There is a danger that in the confrontation between apocalyptic pessimism, on the one hand, and a dismissive smugness, on the other, a
genuine understanding of the nature of the population problem may
be lost.[1]

Visions of impending doom have been increasingly aired in recent
years, often presenting the population problem as a "bomb" that has
been planted and is about to "go off." These catastrophic images have
encouraged a tendency to search for emergency solutions that treat
the people involved not as reasonable beings, allies facing a common
problem, but as impulsive and uncontrolled sources of great social
harm, in need of strong discipline.

Such views have received serious attention in public discussions, not
just in sensational headlines in the popular press, but also in seriously

---

Amartya Sen is Lamont University Professor and professor of economics
and philosophy at Harvard University. This essay appeared in the September
22, 1994, issue of the *New York Review of Books* and is reprinted here by
permission of the author and publisher.

101

argued and widely read books. One of the most influential examples was Paul Ehrlich's *The Population Bomb,* the first three sections of which were headed "Too Many People," "Too Little Food," and "A Dying Planet."[2] A more recent example of a chilling diagnosis of imminent calamity is Garrett Hardin's *Living Within Limits.*[3] The arguments on which these pessimistic visions are based deserve serious scrutiny.

If the propensity to foresee impending disaster from overpopulation is strong in some circles, so is the tendency, in others, to dismiss all worries about population size. Just as alarmism builds on the recognition of a real problem and then magnifies it, complacency may also start off from a reasonable belief about the history of population problems and fail to see how they may have changed by now. It is often pointed out, for example, that the world has coped well enough with fast increases in population in the past, even though alarmists had expected otherwise. Malthus anticipated terrible disasters resulting from population growth and a consequent imbalance in "the proportion between the natural increase of population and food."[4] At a time when there were fewer than a billion people, he was quite convinced that "the period when the number of men surpass their means of subsistence has long since arrived." However, since Malthus first published his famous *Essay on Population* in 1798, the world population has grown nearly six times larger, while food output and consumption per person are considerably higher now, and there has been an unprecedented increase both in life expectancies and in general living standards.[5]

The fact that Malthus was mistaken in his diagnosis as well as his prognosis two hundred years ago does not, however, indicate that contemporary fears about population growth must be similarly erroneous. The increase in the world population has vastly accelerated over the last century. It took the world population millions of years to reach the first billion, then 123 years to get to the second, 33 years to the third, 14 years to the fourth, 13 years to the fifth billion, with a sixth billion to come, according to one U.N. projection, in another 11 years.[6] During the last decade, between 1980 and 1990, the number of people on earth grew by about 923 million, an increase nearly the size of the total world population in Malthus's time. Whatever may be the proper response to alarmism about the future, complacency based on past success is no response at all.

Immigration and Population

One current worry concerns the regional distribution of the increase in world population, about 90 percent of which is taking place in the developing countries. The percentage rate of population growth is fastest in Africa—3.1 percent per year over the last decade. But most of the large increases in population occur in regions other than Africa. The largest absolute increases in numbers are taking place in Asia, which is where most of the world's poorer people live, even though the rate of increase in population has been slowing significantly there. Of the worldwide increase of 923 million people in the 1980s, well over half occurred in Asia—517 million in fact (including 146 million in China and 166 million in India).

Beyond concerns about the well-being of these poor countries themselves, a more self-regarding worry causes panic in the richer countries of the world and has much to do with the current anxiety in the West about the "world population problem." This is founded on the belief that destitution caused by fast population growth in the Third World is responsible for the severe pressure to emigrate to the developed countries of Europe and North America. In this view, people impoverished by overpopulation in the "South" flee to the "North." Some have claimed to find empirical support for this thesis in the fact that pressure to emigrate from the South has accelerated in recent decades, along with a rapid increase in the population there.

There are two distinct questions here: First, how real a threat of intolerable immigration pressure does the North face from the South, and second, is that pressure closely related to population growth in the South, rather than to other social and economic factors? There are reasons to doubt that population growth is the major force behind migratory pressures, and I shall concentrate here on that question. But I should note in passing that immigration is now severely controlled in Europe and North America, and insofar as Europe is concerned, most of the current immigrants from the Third World are not "primary" immigrants but dependent relatives—mainly spouses and young children—of those who had come and settled earlier. The United States remains relatively more open to fresh immigration, but the requirements of "labor certification" as a necessary part of the immigration procedure tend to guarantee that the new entrants are relatively better educated and more skilled. There are, however, sizable flows of illegal immigrants, especially to the United States and to a lesser extent to southern Europe, though the numbers are hard to estimate.

What causes the current pressures to emigrate? The "job-worthy" people who get through the immigration process are hardly to be seen as impoverished and destitute migrants created by the sheer pressure of population. Even the illegal immigrants who manage to evade the rigors of border control are typically not starving wretches but those who can make use of work prospects in the North.

The explanation for the increased migratory pressure over the decades owes more to the dynamism of international capitalism than to just the growing size of the population of the Third World countries. The immigrants have allies in potential employers, and this applies as much to illegal farm laborers in California as to the legally authorized "guest workers" in automobile factories in Germany. The economic incentive to emigrate to the North from the poorer Southern economies may well depend on differences in real income. But this gap is very large anyway, and even if it is presumed that population growth in the South is increasing the disparity with the North—a thesis I shall presently consider—it seems unlikely that this incentive would significantly change if the Northern income level were, say, twenty times that of the Southern as opposed to twenty-five times.

The growing demand for immigration to the North from the South is related to the "shrinking" of the world (through revolutions in communication and transport), reduction in economic obstacles to labor movements (despite the increase in political barriers), and the growing reach and absorptive power of international capitalism (even as domestic politics in the North has turned more inward-looking and nationalistic). To try to explain the increase in immigration pressure by the growth rate of total population in the Third World is to close one's eyes to the deep changes that have occurred—and are occurring—in the world in which we live, and the rapid internationalization of its cultures and economies that accompanies these changes.

Fears of Being Engulfed

A closely related issue concerns what is perceived as a growing "imbalance" in the division of the world population, with a rapidly rising share belonging to the Third World. That fear translates into worries of various kinds in the North, especially the sense of being overrun by the South. Many Northerners fear being engulfed by people from Asia and Africa, whose share of the world population increased from 63.7 percent in 1950 to 71.2 percent by 1990, and is expected, according to the estimates of the United Nations, to rise to 78.5 percent by 2050.

It is easy to understand the fears of relatively well-off people at the thought of being surrounded by a fast-growing and increasingly impoverished Southern population. As I shall argue, the thesis of growing impoverishment does not stand up to much scrutiny; but it is important to address first the psychologically tense issue of racial balance in the world (even though racial composition as a consideration has only as much importance as we choose to give it). Here it is worth recollecting that the Third World is right now going through the same kind of demographic shift—a rapid expansion of population for a temporary but long stretch—that Europe and North America experienced during their Industrial Revolution. In 1650 the share of Asia and Africa in the world population is estimated to have been 78.4 percent, and it stayed around there even in 1750.[7] With the Industrial Revolution, the share of Asia and Africa diminished because of the rapid rise of population in Europe and North America; for example, during the nineteenth century, while the population of Asia and Africa grew by about 4 percent per decade or less, the population of "the area of European settlement" grew by around 10 percent every decade.

Even now the combined share of Asia and Africa (71.2 percent) is considerably *below* what that share was in 1650 or 1750. If the United Nations' prediction that this share will rise to 78.5 percent by 2050 comes true, then the Asians and the Africans would return to being proportionately almost exactly as numerous as they were before the European industrial revolution. There is, of course, nothing sacrosanct about the distributions of population in the past; but the sense of a growing "imbalance" in the world, based only on recent trends, ignores history and implicitly presumes that the expansion of Europeans earlier on was natural, whereas the same process happening now to other populations unnaturally disturbs the "balance."

Collaboration Versus Override

Other worries involving the relation of population growth to food supplies, income levels, and the environment reflect more serious matters.[8] Before I take up those questions, a brief comment on the distinction between two rival approaches to dealing with the population problem may be useful. One involves voluntary choice and a collaborative solution, and the other overrides voluntarism through legal or economic coercion.

Alarmist views of impending crises tend to produce a willingness to consider forceful measures for coercing people to have fewer children in the Third World. Imposing birth control on unwilling people is no longer rejected as readily as it was until quite recently, and some activists have pointed to the ambiguities that exist in determining what is or is not "coercion."[9] Those who are willing to consider—or at least not fully reject—programs that would use some measure of force to reduce population growth often point to the success of China's "one child policy" in cutting down the national birth rate. Force can also take an indirect form, as when economic opportunities are changed so radically by government regulations that people are left with very little choice except to behave in ways the government would approve. In China's case, the government may refuse to offer housing to families with too many children—thus penalizing the children as well as the adults.

In India the policy of compulsory birth control that was initiated during the "emergency period" declared by Mrs. Gandhi in the 1970s was decisively rejected by the voters in the general election in which it—along with civil rights—was a major issue. Even so, some public health clinics in the northern states (such as Uttar Pradesh) insist, in practice, on sterilization before providing normal medical attention to women and men beyond a certain age. The pressures to move in that direction seem to be strong, and they are reinforced by the rhetoric of "the population bomb."

I shall call this general approach the "override" view, since the family's personal decisions are overridden by some agency outside the family—typically by the government of the country in question (whether or not it has been pressed to do so by "outside" agencies, such as international organizations and pressure groups). In fact, overriding is not limited to an explicit use of legal coercion or economic compulsion, since people's own choices can also be effectively overridden by simply not offering them the opportunities for jobs or welfare that they can expect to get from a responsible government. Override can take many different forms and can be of varying intensity (with the Chinese "one child policy" being something of an extreme case of a more general approach).

A central issue here is the increasingly vocal demand by some activists concerned with population growth that the highest "priority" should be given in Third World countries to family planning over other public commitments. This demand goes much beyond supporting family planning as a part of development. In fact, proposals for shifting international aid away from development in general to family planning in particular have lately been increasingly frequent. Such policies fit into the general approach of "override" as well, since they try to rely on manipulating people's choices through offering them only some opportunities (the means of family planning) while denying others, no matter what they would have themselves preferred. Insofar as they would have the effect of reducing health care and educational services, such shifts in public commitments will not only add to the misery of human lives but may also have, I shall argue, exactly the opposite effect on family planning than the one intended, since education and health care have a significant part in the *voluntary* reduction of the birth rate.

The "override" approach contrasts with another, the "collaborative" approach, that relies not on legal or economic restrictions but on rational decisions of women and men, based on expanded choices and enhanced security, and encouraged by open dialogue and extensive public discussions. The difference between the two approaches does not lie in government's activism in the first case as opposed to passivity in the second. Even if solutions are sought through the decisions and actions of people themselves, the chance to take reasoned decisions with more knowledge and a greater sense of personal security can be increased by public policies, for example, through expanding educational facilities, health care, and economic well-being, along with providing better access to family planning. The central political and ethical issue concerning the "override" approach does not lie in its insistence on the need for public policy but in the ways it significantly reduces the choices open to parents.

The Malthus-Condorcet Debate

Thomas Robert Malthus forcefully argued for a version of the "override" view. In fact, it was precisely this preference that distinguished Malthus from Condorcet, the eighteenth-century French mathematician and social scientist from whom Malthus had actually derived the analysis of how population could outgrow the means of living. The debate between Condorcet and Malthus in some ways marks the origin of the distinction between the "collaborative" and the "override" approaches, which still compete for attention.[10]

In his *Essay on Population,* published in 1798, Malthus quoted—extensively and with approval—Condorcet's discussion, in 1795, of the possibility of overpopulation. However, true to the Enlightenment tradition, Condorcet was confident that this problem would be solved by reasoned human action: through increases in productivity, through better conservation and prevention of waste, and through education (especially female education), which would contribute to reducing the birth rate.[11] Voluntary family planning would be encouraged, in Condorcet's analysis, by increased understanding that if people "have a duty toward those who are not yet born, that duty is not to give them existence but to give them happiness." They would see the value of limiting family size "rather than foolishly . . . encumber the world with useless and wretched beings."[12]

Even though Malthus borrowed from Condorcet his diagnosis of the possibility of overpopulation, he refused to accept Condorcet's solution. Indeed, Malthus's essay on population was partly a criticism of Condorcet's Enlightenment reasoning, and the full title of Malthus's famous essay specifically mentioned Condorcet. Malthus argued that "there is no reason whatever to suppose anything beside the difficulty of procuring in adequate plenty the necessaries of life should either *indispose* this greater number of persons to marry early, or *disable* them from rearing in health the largest families."[13] Malthus thus opposed public relief of poverty: he saw the "poor laws" in particular as contributing greatly to population growth.[14]

Malthus was not sure that any public policy would work, and whether "overriding" would in fact be possible: "The perpetual tendency in the race of man to increase beyond the means of subsistence is one of the great general laws of animated nature which we can have no reason to expect will change."[15] But insofar as any solution would be possible, it could not come from voluntary decisions of the people involved, acting from a position of strength and economic security. It must come from overriding their preferences through the compulsions of economic necessity, since their poverty was the only thing that could "indispose this greater number of persons to marry early, or disable them from rearing in health the largest families."

Development and Lower Fertility

The distinction between the "collaborative" approach and the "override" approach thus tends to correspond closely to the contrast between, on the one hand, treating economic and social development as the way to solve the population problem and, on the other, expecting little from development and using, instead, legal and economic pressures to reduce birth rates. Among recent writers, those such as Gerard Piel[16] who have persuasively emphasized our ability to solve problems through reasoned decisions and actions have tended—like Condorcet—to find the solution of the population problem in economic and social conditions favoring slower population growth. In contrast, those who have been thoroughly skeptical of reasoned human action to limit population growth have tended to go in the direction of "override" in one form or another, rather than concentrate on development and voluntarism.

Has development, in fact, done much to reduce population growth? There can be little doubt that economic and social development, in general, has been associated with major reductions in birth rates and the emergence of smaller families as the norm. This is a pattern that was, of course, clearly observed in Europe and North America as they underwent industrialization, but that experience has been repeated in many other parts of the world.

In particular, conditions of economic security and affluence, wider availability of contraceptive methods, expansion of education (particularly female education), and lower mortality rates have had—and are currently having—quite substantial effects in reducing birth rates in different parts of the world.[17] The rate of world population growth is certainly declining, and even over the last two decades its percentage growth rate has fallen from 2.2 percent per year between 1970 and

1980 to 1.7 percent between 1980 and 1992. This rate is expected to go steadily down until the size of the world's population becomes nearly stationary.[18]

There are important regional differences in demographic behavior; for example, the population growth rate in India peaked at 2.2 percent a year (in the 1970s) and has since started to diminish, whereas most Latin American countries peaked at much higher rates before coming down sharply, while many countries in Africa currently have growth rates between 3 and 4 percent, with an average for sub-Saharan Africa of 3.1 percent. Similarly, the different factors have varied in their respective influence from region to region. But there can be little dispute that economic and social development tends to reduce fertility rates. The regions of the Third World that lag most in achieving economic and social development, such as many countries in Africa, are, in general, also the ones that have failed to reduce birth rates significantly. Malthus's fear that economic and social development could only encourage people to have more children has certainly proved to be radically wrong, and so have all the painful policy implications drawn from it.

This raises the following question: In view of the clear connection between development and lower fertility, why isn't the dispute over how to deal with population growth fully resolved already? Why don't we reinterpret the population problem simply as a problem of underdevelopment (even if we reject the oversimple slogan "development is the most reliable contraceptive")?

In the long run, this may indeed be exactly the right approach. The problem is more complex, however, because a "contraceptive" that is "reliable" in the long run may not act fast enough to meet the present threat. Even though development may dependably work to stabilize population if it is given enough time, there may not be, it is argued, time enough to give. The death rate often falls very fast with more widely available health care, better sanitation, and improved nutrition, while the birth rate may fall rather slowly. Much growth of population may meanwhile occur.

This is exactly the point at which apocalyptic prophecies add force to the "override" view. One claim, then, that needs examination is that the world is facing an imminent crisis, one so urgent that development is just too slow a process to deal with it. We must try right now, the argument goes, to cut down population growth by drastic and forceful means if necessary. The second claim that also needs scrutiny is the actual feasibility of adequately reducing population growth through these drastic means, without fostering social and economic development.

POPULATION AND INCOME

It is sometimes argued that signs of an imminent crisis can be found in the growing impoverishment of the South, with falling income per capita accompanying high population growth. In general, there is little evidence for this. As a matter of fact, the average population of "low income" countries (as defined by the World Bank) has been enjoying not only a rising gross national product (GNP) per capita, but a growth rate of GNP per capita (3.9 percent per year for 1980-92) that is much faster than the rates for the "high income" countries (2.4 percent) and the "middle income" ones (0 percent).[19]

The growth of per capita GNP of the population of low-income countries would have been even higher had it not been for the negative growth rates of many countries in sub-Saharan Africa, one region in which a number of countries have been experiencing economic decline. But the main culprit causing this state of affairs is the terrible failure of economic production in sub-Saharan Africa (connected particularly with political disruption, including wars and military rule), rather than population growth, which is only a subsidiary factor. Sub-Saharan Africa does have high population growth, but its economic stagnation has contributed much more to the fall in its per capita income.

With its average population growth rate of 3.1 percent per year, had sub-Saharan Africa suddenly matched China's low population growth of 1.4 percent (the lowest among the low-income countries), it would have gained roughly 1.7 percent in per capita GNP growth. The real income per person would still have fallen, even with that minimal population growth, for many countries in the region. The growth of GNP per capita is *minus* 1.9 percent for Ethiopia, *minus* 1.8 percent for Togo, *minus* 3.6 percent for Mozambique, *minus* 4.3 percent for Niger, *minus* 4.7 percent for Ivory Coast, not to mention Somalia,

Sudan, and Angola, where the political disruption has been so serious that no reliable GNP estimates even exist. A lower population growth rate could have reduced the magnitude of the fall in per capita GNP, but the main roots of Africa's economic decline lie elsewhere. The complex political factors underlying the troubles of Africa include, among other things, the subversion of democracy and the rise of combative military rulers, often encouraged by the Cold War (with Africa providing "client states"—from Somalia and Ethiopia to Angola and Zaire—for the superpowers, particularly from the 1960s onward). The explanation of sub-Saharan Africa's problems has to be sought in these political troubles, which affect economic stability, agricultural and industrial incentives, public health arrangements, and social services—even family planning and population policy.[20]

There is indeed a very powerful case for reducing the rate of growth of population in Africa, but this problem cannot be dissociated from the rest of the continent's woes. Sub-Saharan Africa lags behind other developing regions in economic security, in health care, in life expectancy, in basic education, and in political and economic stability. It should be no great surprise that it lags behind in family planning as well. To dissociate the task of population control from the politics and economics of Africa would be a great mistake and would seriously mislead public policy.

Population and Food Production

Malthus's exact thesis cannot, however, be disputed by quoting statistics of income per capita, for he was concerned specifically with food supply per capita, and he concentrated on "the proportion between the natural increase of population and food." Many modern commentators, including Paul Ehrlich and Garrett Hardin, have said much about this, too. When Ehrlich says, in his *Population Bomb*, "too little food," he does not mean "too little income," but specifically a growing shortage of food.

Is population beginning to outrun food production? Even though such an impression is often given in public discussions, there is, in fact, no serious evidence that this is happening. While there are some year-to-year fluctuations in the growth of food output (typically inducing, whenever things slacken a bit, some excited remarks by those who sense an impending doom), the worldwide trend of food output per person has been firmly upward. Not only over the two centuries since Malthus's time, but also during recent decades, the rise in food output has been significantly and consistently outpacing the expansion of world population.[21]

But the total food supply in the world as a whole is not the only issue. What about the regional distribution of food? If it were to turn out that the rising ratio of food to population is mainly caused by increased production in richer countries (for example, if it appeared that the U.S. wheat output was feeding the Third World, in which much of the population expansion is taking place), then the neo-Malthusian fears about "too many people" and "too little food" may have some plausibility. Is this what is happening?

In fact, with one substantial exception, exactly the opposite is true. The largest increases in the production of food—not just in the aggregate but also per person—are actually taking place in the Third World, particularly in the region that is having the largest absolute increases in the world population, that is, in Asia. The many millions of people who are added to the populations of India and China may be constantly cited by the terrorized—and terrorizing—advocates of the apocalyptic view, but it is precisely in these countries that the most rapid rates of growth in food output per capita are to be observed. For example, between the three-year averages of 1979-81 and 1991-93, food production per capita in the world moved up by 3 percent, while it went up by only 2 percent in Europe and went down by nearly 5 percent in North America. In contrast, per capita food production jumped up by 22 percent in Asia generally, including 23 percent in India and 39 percent in China.[22] (See Table 1, p. 114.)

During the same period, however, food production per capita went down by 6 percent in Africa, and even the absolute size of food output fell in some countries (such as Malawi and Somalia). Of course, many countries in the world—from Syria, Italy, and Sweden to Botswana in Africa—have had declining food production per capita without experiencing hunger, since their economies have prospered and grown; when the means are available, food can be easily bought in the international market. For many countries in sub-Saharan Africa, the problem arises from the fact that the decline in food production is an integral part of the story of overall economic decline, which I discussed earlier.

TABLE 1   Indices of Food Production Per Capita

	1979-81 Base Period	1991-93
World	100	103
Europe	100	102
North America	100	95
Africa	100	94
Asia	100	122
including		
India	100	123
China	100	139

Source: FAO Quarterly Bulletin of Statistics

Difficulties of food production in sub-Saharan Africa, like other problems of the national economy, are not only linked to wars, dictatorships, and political chaos. In addition, there is some evidence that climatic shifts have had unfavorable effects on parts of that continent. While some of the climatic problems may be caused partly by increases in human settlement and environmental neglect, that neglect is not unrelated to the political and economic chaos that has characterized sub-Saharan Africa during the last few decades. The food problem of Africa must be seen as one part of a wider political and economic problem in the region.[23]

The Declining Price of Food

To return to the balance between food and population: rising food production per capita in the world as a whole, and in the Third World in particular, contradicts some of the pessimism that characterized the gloomy predictions of the past. Prophecies of imminent disaster during the last few decades have not proved any more accurate than Malthus's prognostication nearly two hundred years ago. As for new prophecies of doom, they cannot, of course, be contradicted until the future arrives. There was no way of refuting the theses of W. Paddock and P. Paddock's popular book *Famine—1975!*, published in 1968, which predicted a terrible cataclysm for the world as a whole by 1975 (writing of India, in particular, as a basket case), until 1975 actually arrived. The new prophets have learned not to attach specific dates to the crises they foresee, and past failures do not seem to have reduced the popular appetite for this creative genre.

However, after noting the rather dismal forecasting record of doomsayers, we must also accept the general methodological point that present trends in output do not necessarily tell us much about the prospects of further expansion. It could, for example, be argued that maintaining growth in food production may require proportionately increasing investments of capital, drawing them away from other kinds of production. This would tend to make food progressively more expensive if there are "diminishing returns" in shifting resources from other fields into food production. And, ultimately, further expansion of food production may become so expensive that it would be hard to maintain the trend of increasing food production without reducing other outputs drastically.

But is food production really getting more and more expensive? There is, in fact, no evidence for that conclusion either. In fact, quite the contrary. Not only is food generally much cheaper to buy today, in constant dollars, than it was in Malthus's time, but it also has become cheaper during recent decades. As a matter of fact, there have been increasing complaints among food exporters, especially in the Third World, that food prices have fallen in relation to other commodities. For example, in 1992 a United Nations report recorded a 38 percent fall in the relative prices of "basic foods" over the last decade.[24] This is entirely in line with the trend, during the last three decades, toward declining relative prices of particular food items, in relation to the prices of manufactured goods. The World Bank's adjusted estimates of the prices of particular food crops, between 1953-55 and 1983-85, show similarly steep declines for such staples as rice (42 percent), wheat (57 percent), sorghum (39 percent), and maize (37 percent).[25]

Not only is food getting less expensive, but we also have to bear in mind that the current increase in food production (substantial and well ahead of population growth, as it is) is itself being kept in check by the difficulties in selling food profitably as the relative prices of food have fallen. Those neo-Malthusians who concede that food production is now growing faster than population often point out that it is growing "only a little faster than population," and they are inclined to interpret this as evidence that we are reaching the limits of what we can produce to keep pace with population growth.

But surely that is the wrong conclusion to draw in view of the falling relative prices of food, and the current difficulties in selling food, since it ignores the effects of economic incentives that govern production. When we take into account the persistent cheapening of food prices, we have good grounds to suggest that food output is being held back by a lack of effective demand in the market. The imaginary crisis in food production, contradicted as it is by the upward trends of total and regional food output per capita, is thus further debunked by an analysis of the economic incentives to produce more food.

Population and Deprivation

I have examined the alleged "food problem" associated with population growth in some detail because it has received so much attention both in the traditional Malthusian literature and in the recent writings of neo-Malthusians. In concentrating on his claim that growing populations would not have enough food, Malthus differed from Condorcet's broader presentation of the population question. Condorcet's own emphasis was on the possibility of "a continual diminution of happiness" as a result of population growth, a diminution that could occur in many different ways—not just through the deprivation of food, but through a decline in living conditions generally. That more extensive worry can remain even when Malthus's analysis of food supply is rejected.

Indeed, average income and food production per capita can go on increasing even as the wretchedly deprived living conditions of particular sections of the population get worse, as they have in many parts of the Third World. The living conditions of backward regions and deprived classes can decline even when a country's economic growth is very rapid on the average. Brazil during the 1960s and 1970s provided an extreme example of this. The sense that there are just "too many people" around often arises from seeing the desperate lives of people in the large and rapidly growing urban slums—*bidonvilles*—in poor countries, sobering reminders that we should not take too much comfort from aggregate statistics of economic progress.

But in an essay addressed mainly to the population problem, what we have to ask is not whether things are just fine in the Third World (they obviously are not), but whether population growth is the root cause of the deprivation that people suffer. The question is whether the particular instances of deep poverty we observe derive mainly from population growth rather than from other factors that lead to unshared prosperity and persistent and possibly growing inequality. The tendency to see in population growth an explanation for every calamity that afflicts poor people is now fairly well established in some circles, and the message that gets transmitted constantly is the opposite of the old picture postcard: "Wish you weren't here."

To see in population growth the main reason for the growth of overcrowded and very poor slums in large cities, for example, is not empirically convincing. It does not help to explain why the slums of Calcutta and Bombay have grown worse at a faster rate than those of Karachi and Islamabad (India's population growth rate is 2.1 percent per year, Pakistan's 3.1), or why Jakarta has deteriorated faster than Ankara or Istanbul (Indonesian population growth is 1.8 percent, Turkey's 2.3), or why the slums of Mexico City have become worse more rapidly than those of San José (Mexico's population growth rate is 2.0, Costa Rica's 2.8), or why Harlem can seem more and more deprived when compared with the poorer districts of Singapore (U.S. population growth rate is 1.0, Singapore's is 1.8). Many causal factors affect the degree of deprivation in particular parts of a country—rural as well as urban—and to try to see them all as resulting from overpopulation is the negation of social analysis.

This is not to deny that population growth may well have an effect on deprivation, but only to insist that any investigation of the effects of population growth must be part of the analysis of economic and political processes, including the effects of other variables. It is the isolationist view of population growth that should be rejected.

Threats to the Environment

In his concern about "a continual diminution of happiness" from population growth, Condorcet was a pioneer in considering the possibility that natural raw materials might be used up, thereby making living conditions worse. In his characteristically rationalist solution, which relied partly on voluntary and reasoned measures to reduce the birth rate, Condorcet also envisaged the development of less improvident technology: "The manufacture of articles will be achieved with less wastage in raw materials and will make better use of them."[26]

The effects of a growing population on the environment could be a good deal more serious than the food problems that have received so much attention in the literature inspired by Malthus. If the environment is damaged by population pressures, this obviously affects the kind of life we lead, and the possibilities of a "diminution in happiness" can be quite considerable.

In dealing with this problem, we have to distinguish once again between the long and the short run. The short-run picture tends to be dominated by the fact that the per capita consumption of food, fuel, and other goods by people in Third World countries is often relatively low; consequently the impact of population growth in these countries is not, in relative terms, so damaging to the global environment. But the problems of the local environment can, of course, be serious in many developing economies. They vary from the "neighborhood pollution" created by unregulated industries to the pressure of denser populations on rural resources such as fields and woods.[27] (The Indian authorities had to close down several factories in and around Agra, since the facade of the Taj Mahal was turning pale as a result of chemical pollution from local factories.) But it remains true that one additional American typically has a larger negative impact on the ozone layer, global warmth, and other elements of the earth's environment than dozens of Indians and Zimbabweans put together. Those who argue for the immediate need for forceful population control in the Third World to preserve the global environment must first recognize this elementary fact.

This does not imply, as is sometimes suggested, that as far as the global environment is concerned, population growth in the Third World is nothing to worry about. The long-run impact on the global environment of population growth in the developing countries can be expected to be large. As the Indians and the Zimbabweans develop economically, they too will consume a great deal more, and they will pose, in the future, a threat to the earth's environment similar to that of people in the rich countries today. The long-run threat of population to the environment is a real one.

WOMEN'S WELL-BEING AND FERTILITY

Since reducing the birth rate can be slow, this and other long-run problems should be addressed right now. Solutions will no doubt have to be found in the two directions to which, as it happens, Condorcet pointed: (1) developing new technology and new behavior patterns that would waste little and pollute less, and (2) fostering social and economic changes that would gradually bring down the growth rate of population.

On reducing birth rates, Condorcet's own solution not only included enhancing economic opportunity and security, but also stressed the importance of education, particularly female education. A better-educated population could have a more informed discussion of the kind of life we have reason to value; in particular it would reject the drudgery of a life of continuous childbearing and child-rearing that is routinely forced on many Third World women. That drudgery, in some ways, is the most immediate consequence of high fertility rates.

Central to reducing birth rates, then, is a close connection between women's well-being and their power to make their own decisions and bring about changes in the fertility pattern. Women in many Third World countries are deprived by high birth frequency of the freedom to do other things in life, not to mention the medical dangers of repeated pregnancy and high maternal mortality, which are both characteristic of many developing countries. It is thus not surprising that reductions in birth rates have typically been associated with improvement of women's status and their ability to make their voices heard—often the result of expanded opportunities for schooling and political activity.[28]

There is nothing particularly exotic about declines in the birth rate occurring through a process of voluntary rational assessment, of which Condorcet spoke. It is what people do when they have some basic education, know about family-planning methods and have access to them, do not readily accept a life of persistent drudgery, and are not deeply anxious about their economic security. It is also what they do when they are not forced by high infant—and child—mortality rates to be so worried that no child will survive to support them in their old age that they try to have many children. In country after country the birth rate has come down with more female education, the reduction of mortality rates, the expansion of economic means and security, and greater public discussion of ways of living.

Is Gradualism Good Enough?

There is little doubt that this process of social and economic change will over time cut down the birth rate. Indeed the growth rate of world population is already firmly declining—it came down from 2.2 percent in the 1970s to 1.7 percent between 1980 and 1992. Had imminent cataclysm been threatening, we might have had good reason to reject such gradual progress and consider more drastic means of population control, as some have advocated. But that apocalyptic view is empirically baseless. There is no imminent emergency that calls for a breathless response. What is called for is systematic support for people's own decisions to reduce family size through expanding education and health care, and through economic and social development.

It is often asked where the money needed for expanding education, health care, and the like would be found. Education, health services, and many other means of improving the quality of life are typically highly labor-intensive in poor countries (because of low wages).[29] While poor countries have less money to spend, they also need less money to provide these services. For this reason many poor countries have indeed been able to expand educational and health services widely without waiting to become prosperous through the process of economic growth. Sri Lanka, Costa Rica, Indonesia, and Thailand are good examples, and there are many others. While the impact of these social services on the quality and length of life has been much studied, they are also major means of reducing the birth rate.

CHINA'S POPULATION POLICIES

By contrast with such open and voluntary developments, coercive methods, such as the "one child policy" in some regions, have been tried in China, particularly since the reforms of 1979. Many commentators have pointed out that by 1992 the Chinese birth rate had fallen to 19 per 1,000, compared with 29 per 1,000 in India, and 37 per 1,000 for the average of other poor countries other than China and India.

China's total fertility rate (reflecting the number of children born per woman) is now at "the replacement level" of 2.0, compared with India's 3.6 and the weighted average of 4.9 for low-income countries other than China and India.[30] Hasn't China shown the way to "solve" the population problem in other developing countries as well?

The difficulties with this "solution" are of several kinds. First, if freedom is valued at all, the lack of freedom associated with this approach must be seen to be a social loss in itself. The importance of reproductive freedom has been persuasively emphasized by women's groups throughout the world.[31]

The loss of freedom is often dismissed on grounds that because of cultural differences, authoritarian policies that would not be tolerated in the West are acceptable to Asians. While we often hear references to "despotic" Oriental traditions, such arguments are no more convincing than a claim that compulsion in the West is justified by the traditions of the Spanish Inquisition or of the Nazi concentration camps. Frequent references are also made to the emphasis on discipline in the "Confucian tradition"; but that is not the only tradition for modern Asia (even if we were able to show that discipline is more important for Confucius than it is for, say, Plato or Saint Augustine).

Only a democratic expression of opinion could reveal whether citizens would find a compulsory system acceptable. While such a test has not occurred in China, one did in fact take place in India during "the emergency period" in the 1970s, when Indira Gandhi's government imposed compulsory birth control and suspended various legal freedoms. In the general elections that followed, the politicians favoring the policy of coercion were overwhelmingly defeated. Furthermore, family-planning experts in India have observed how the briefly applied programs of compulsory sterilization tended to discredit voluntary birth-control programs generally, since people became deeply suspicious of the entire movement to control fertility.

Second, apart from the fundamental issue of whether people are willing to accept compulsory birth control, its specific consequences must also be considered. Insofar as coercion is effective, it works by making people do things they would not freely do. The social consequences of such compulsion, including the ways in which an unwilling population tends to react when it is coerced, can be appalling. For example, the demands of a "one-child family" can lead to the neglect—or worse—of a second child, thereby increasing the infant-mortality rate. Moreover, in a country with a strong preference for male children—a preference shared by China and many other countries in Asia and North Africa—a policy of allowing only one child per family can easily lead to the fatal neglect of a female child. There is much evidence that this is fairly widespread in China, with very adverse effects on infant-mortality rates. There are reports that female children have been severely neglected as well as suggestions that female infanticide occurs with considerable frequency. Such consequences are hard to tolerate morally, and perhaps politically also, in the long run.

Third, what is also not clear is exactly how much additional reduction in the birth rate has been achieved through these coercive methods. Many of China's longstanding social and economic programs have been valuable in reducing fertility, including those that have expanded education for women as well as men, made health care more generally available, provided more job opportunities for women, and stimulated rapid economic growth. These factors would themselves have reduced the birth rate, and it is not clear how much "extra lowering" of fertility rates has been achieved in China through compulsion.

For example, we can determine whether many of the countries that match (or outmatch) China in life expectancy, female literacy rates, and female participation in the labor force actually have a higher fertility rate than China. Of all the countries in the world for which data are given in the World Development Report 1994, there are only three such countries: Jamaica (2.7), Thailand (2.2), and Sweden (2.1) —and the fertility rates of two of these are close to China's (2.0). Thus the additional contribution of coercion to reducing fertility in China is by no means clear, since compulsion was superimposed on a society that was already reducing its birth rate and in which education and jobs outside the home were available to large numbers of women. In some regions of China the compulsory program needed little enforcement, whereas in other—more backward—regions, it had to be applied with much severity, with terrible consequences in infant mortality and discrimination against female children. While China may get too much credit for its authoritarian measures, it gets far too little credit for the other more collaborative and participatory policies it has followed, which have themselves helped to cut the birth rate.

Comparing China and India

A useful contrast can be drawn between China and India, the two most populous countries in the world. If we look only at the national averages, it is easy to see that China with its low fertility rate of 2.0 has achieved much more than India has with its average fertility rate of 3.6. To what extent this contrast can be attributed to the effectiveness of the coercive policies used in China is not clear, since we would expect the fertility rate to be much lower in China in view of its higher percentage of female literacy (almost twice as high), higher life expectancy (almost ten years more), larger female involvement (by three quarters) in the labor force, and so on.

But India is a country of great diversity, whose different states have very unequal achievements in literacy, health care, and economic and social development. Most states in India are far behind the Chinese provinces in educational achievement (with the exception of Tibet, which has the lowest literacy rate of any Chinese or Indian state), and the same applies to other factors that affect fertility. However, the state of Kerala in southern India provides an interesting comparison with China, since it too has high levels of basic education, health care, and so on. Kerala is a state within a country, but with its 29 million people, it is larger than most countries in the world (including Canada). Kerala's birth rate of 18 per 1,000 is actually lower than China's 19 per 1,000, and its fertility rate is 1.8 for 1991, compared with China's 2.0 for 1992. These low rates have been achieved without any state coercion.[32]

The roots of Kerala's success are to be found in the kinds of social progress Condorcet hoped for, including, among others, a high female literacy rate (86 percent, which is substantially higher than China's 68 percent). The rural literacy rate is in fact higher in Kerala—for women as well as men—than in every single province in China. Male and female life expectancies at birth in China are respectively 67 and 71 years; the provisional 1991 figures for men and women in Kerala are 71 and 74 years. Women have been active in Kerala's economic and political life for a long time. A high proportion do skilled and semi-skilled work, and a large number have taken part in educational movements.[33] It is perhaps of symbolic importance that the first public pronouncement of the need for widespread elementary education in any part of India was made in 1817 by Rani Gouri Parvathi Bai, the young queen of the princely state of Travancore, which makes up a substantial part of modern Kerala. For a long time public discussions in Kerala have centered on women's rights and the undesirability of couples' marrying when very young.

This political process has been voluntary and collaborative, rather than coercive, and the adverse reactions that have been observed in China, such as infant mortality, have not occurred in Kerala. Kerala's low fertility rate has been achieved along with an infant-mortality rate of 16.5 per 1,000 live births (17 for boys and 16 for girls), compared with China's 31 (28 for boys and 33 for girls). And as a result of greater gender equality in Kerala, women have not suffered from higher mortality rates than men in Kerala, as they have in the rest of India and in China, Even the ratio of females to males in the total population in Kerala (above 1.03) is quite close to that of the current ratios in Europe and America (reflecting the usual pattern of lower female mortality whenever women and men receive similar care). By contrast, the average female to male ratio in China is 0.94 and in India as a whole 0.93.[34] Anyone drawn to the Chinese experience of compulsory birth control must take note of these facts.

The temptation to use the "override" approach arises at least partly from impatience with the allegedly slow process of fertility reduction through collaborative, rather than coercive, attempts. Yet Kerala's birth rate has fallen from 44 per 1,000 in the 1950s to 18 by 1991—not a sluggish decline. Nor is Kerala unique in this respect. Other societies, such as those of Sri Lanka, South Korea, and Thailand, which have relied on expanding education and reducing mortality rates—instead of on coercion—have also achieved sharp declines in fertility and birth rates.

It is also interesting to compare the time required for reducing fertility in China with that in the two states in India, Kerala and Tamil Nadu, which have done most to encourage voluntary and collaborative reduction in birth rates (even though Tamil Nadu is well behind Kerala in each respect).[35] Table 2 (p. 125) shows the fertility rates both in 1979, when the one-child policy and related programs were introduced in China, and in 1991. Despite China's one-child policy and other coercive measures, its fertility rate seems to have fallen much less sharply than those of Kerala and Tamil Nadu. The "override"

TABLE 2 Fertility Rates in China and Two Indian States

	1979	1991
China	2.8	2.0
Kerala	3.0	1.8
Tamil Nadu	3.5	2.2

Sources: For China, Xizhe Peng, *Demographic Transition in China* (Oxford University Press, 1991), Li Chengrui, *A Study of China's Population* (Beijing: Foreign Language Press, 1992), and *World Development Report 1994*. For India, *Sample Registration System 1979-80* (New Delhi: Ministry of Home Affairs, 1982) and *Sample Registration System: Fertility and Mortality Indicators 1991* (New Delhi: Ministry of Home Affairs, 1993).

view is very hard to defend on the basis of the Chinese experience, the only systematic and sustained attempt to impose such a policy that has so far been made.

Priority to Family Planning?

Even those who do not advocate legal or economic coercion sometimes suggest a variant of the "override" approach—the view, which has been getting increasing support, that the highest priority should be given simply to family planning, even if this means diverting resources from education and health care as well as other activities associated with development. We often hear claims that enormous declines in birth rates have been accomplished through making family-planning services available, without waiting for improvements in education and health care.

The experience of Bangladesh is sometimes cited as an example of such success. Indeed, even though the female literacy rate in Bangladesh is only around 22 percent and life expectancy at birth no higher than 55 years, fertility rates have been substantially reduced there through the greater availability of family-planning services, including counseling.[36] We have to examine carefully what lessons can, in fact, be drawn from this evidence.

First, it is certainly significant that Bangladesh has been able to cut its fertility rate from 7.0 to 4.5 during the short period between 1975 and 1990, an achievement that discredits the view that people will not voluntarily embrace family planning in the poorest countries. But we have to ask further whether family-planning efforts may themselves be sufficient to make fertility come down to really low levels, without providing for female education and the other features of a fuller collaborative approach. The fertility rate of 4.5 in Bangladesh is still quite high—considerably higher than even India's average rate of 3.6. To begin stabilizing the population, the fertility rates would have to come down closer to the "replacement level" of 2.0, as has happened in Kerala and Tamil Nadu and in many other places outside the Indian subcontinent. Female education and the other social developments connected with lowering the birth rate would still be much needed.

Contrasts between the records of Indian states offer some substantial lessons here. While Kerala, and to a smaller extent Tamil Nadu, have surged ahead in achieving radically reduced fertility rates, other states in India in the so-called northern heartland (such as Uttar Pradesh, Bihar, Madhya Pradesh, and Rajasthan) have very low levels of education, and of general health care (often combined with pressure on the poor to accept birth-control measures, including sterilization, as a qualifying condition for medical attention and other public services). These states all have high fertility rates—between 4.4 and 5.1. The regional contrasts within India strongly argue for the collaborative approach, including active and educated participation of women.

The threat of an impending population crisis tempts many international observers to suggest that priority be given to family-planning arrangements in the Third World countries over other commitments such as education and health care, a redirection of public efforts that is often recommended by policy-makers and at international conferences. Not only will this shift have negative effects on people's well-being and reduce their freedoms, but it can also be self-defeating if the goal is to stabilize population.

The appeal of such slogans as "family planning first" rests partly on misconceptions about what is needed to reduce fertility rates, but also on mistaken beliefs about the excessive costs of social development, including education and health care. As has been discussed, both these activities are highly labor intensive, and thus relatively inexpensive even in very poor economies. In fact, Kerala, India's star performer in expanding education and reducing both death rates and birth rates, is among the poorer Indian states. Its domestically produced income is quite low—lower indeed in per capita terms than even the Indian average—even if this is somewhat deceptive, for the greatest expansion of Kerala's earnings derives from citizens who work outside the state. Kerala's ability to finance adequately both educational expansion and health coverage depends on both activities being labor-intensive; they can be made available even in a low-income economy where there is the political will to use them. Despite its economic backwardness, an issue that Kerala will undoubtedly have to address before long (perhaps by reducing bureaucratic controls over agriculture and industry, which have stagnated), its level of social development has been remarkable, and that has turned out to be crucial in reducing fertility rates. Kerala's fertility rate of 1.8 compares well not only with China's 2.0 but also with the U.S.'s and Sweden's 2.1, Canada's 1.9, and Britain's and France's 1.8.

The population problem is serious, certainly, but neither because of "the proportion between the natural increase of population and food" nor because of some impending apocalypse. There are reasons for worry about the long-term effects of population growth on the environment; and there are strong reasons for concern about the adverse effects of high birth rates on the quality of life, especially of women. With greater opportunities for education (especially female education), reduction of mortality rates (especially of children), improvement in economic security (especially in old age), and greater participation of women in employment and in political action, fast reductions in birth rates can be expected to result through the decisions and actions of those whose lives depend on them.

This is happening right now in many parts of the world, and the result has been a considerable slowing down of world population growth. The best way of dealing with the population problem is to help speed these processes elsewhere. In contrast, the emergency mentality based on false beliefs in imminent cataclysms leads to breathless responses that are deeply counterproductive, preventing the development of rational and sustainable family planning. Coercive policies of forced birth control involve terrible social sacrifices, and there is little evidence that they are more effective in reducing birth rates than serious programs of collaborative action.

5

What Really Happened at Cairo, and Why

George Weigel

Gargantuan international conferences replete with diplomats, "international civil servants," representatives of various "nongovernmental organizations" (NGOs), and the world press have been a staple feature of world politics since the Second World War. One does not fear sinning against charity by suggesting that many of these extravaganzas—in which the international ruling class cavorts, off-hours, in the sybaritic style to which it has become accustomed—are, in the words of the Bard, a "tale told by an idiot, full of sound and fury, signifying nothing."

But there are exceptions, and they can be important. The Helsinki Conference on Security and Cooperation in Europe, which produced the "Helsinki Accords" in 1975, was one such exception. When Leonid Brezhnev signed the Helsinki Final Act in 1975, he probably thought he was taking out a 99-year lease on Stalin's external empire. As things turned out, he was signing its death warrant. For "Basket Three" of the Final Act pledged the signatory nations of Europe and North America to certain human-rights commitments that inspired the formation of "Helsinki monitoring groups." These became the

---

George Weigel is the president of the Ethics and Public Policy Center. He has written or edited fourteen books on religion and public life.

backbone of the human-rights resistance in central and eastern Europe in the late 1970s and throughout the 1980s and played a considerable role in the non-violent collapse of Communism in the Revolution of 1989 and the New Russian Revolution of 1991.[1]

The September 1994 International Conference on Population and Development in Cairo could be another exception, with another ironic outcome. The U.N. bureaucrats, Scandinavian politicos, Clinton administration "global affairs" mavens, radical environmentalists, feminists, and population-controllers who planned the conference intended it to be nothing less than the Great Cairo Turkey Shoot: a political slaughter in which the enemies of "individual autonomy," "sustainable growth," "global carrying capacity," "reproductive rights," "gender equity," abortion-on-demand, and the sexual revolution would be utterly, decisively routed. They were not. Indeed, the Cairo Conference just may have marked a turning point in the international debate over population and development. It is too early to know for sure. But the possibility exists that the radicals' attempt to take the Cairo Conference by storm set in motion moral and cultural dynamics that will, over time, result in the defeat of the radicals' agenda.

FROM BUCHAREST TO PREP-COM III

Cairo was the third in a series of decennial international population conferences. The first International Conference on Population was held in 1974 in Bucharest, and the second (under the enlarged thematic banner of "Population and Development") in 1984 in Mexico City. The planning for both of these meetings, within the U.N. bureaucracy and among the thousands of NGO activists who participate in U.N.-sponsored programs, was dominated by strident doomsayers and hard-core population-controllers of the Garrett Hardin/Paul Ehrlich ("The battle to feed all humanity is over") school. That people were essentially a problem, even a pollutant, rather than a resource, and that social, political, economic, and ecological catastrophe was right around the corner, unless drastic steps were taken to stabilize and then reverse world population trends—these were the themes, familiar to even the casual observer of the American anti-natalist lobby, that set the agenda for Bucharest and Mexico City.

But these analyses, and the prescriptions for coercive, governmentally enforced programs of fertility reduction that flowed from them, did not sit well with many of the putative beneficiaries of "population control," namely, the countries of the developing world. At Bucharest, for example, the population technocrats were challenged both empirically and culturally: empirically, in that it was made plain that, owing to a complex interaction of economic, social, and cultural factors, population patterns varied widely around the world; culturally, in that it became clear that there were many different understandings of how population issues should be addressed, even among those who believed that there indeed was a "population problem." "Development is the best contraceptive" became the slogan that the Third World counterposed to the Hardin/Ehrlich anti-natalist rhetoric of the well-to-do "North."

The population-controllers suffered another defeat at Mexico City. Not satisfied with the results of their massive efforts to export to the Third World mechanical and chemical means of contraception (some of which had met considerable resistance on both moral-cultural and medical grounds), U.N. and private-sector population agencies had increasingly turned to abortion as a means of family planning and population control. The draconian Chinese policy of coercive abortion was only the cruelest face of a practice actively supported by the anti-natalists throughout the developing world.[2] The population-controllers came to Mexico City expecting the conference to give its sanction to abortion-on-demand, in the name of family planning. Yet they were soundly rebuffed. For the conference, with vigorous support from the Reagan administration, adopted a final report that stated flatly that abortion was not a legitimate means of population control.

This was an ideological defeat for the population-controllers, not least because the attention focused on the brutality of the Chinese program graphically demonstrated the lengths to which the controllers were willing to go. Having seen what could be at the end of the road, some countries were prepared to question the legitimacy of embarking on the journey in the first place. The Mexico City conference also had serious financial consequences. Restrictions were placed on funding for abortion in U.N. programs; abortion-funding was eliminated from the population components of many nations' foreign-aid budgets; and, on the domestic front, the Reagan and Bush administrations cited Mexico City as a warrant for prohibiting federal support for any public or private aid program that included abortion among its family-planning activities.

As may be imagined, all of this stuck in the craw of the population-controllers at the U.N. and World Bank, and among the major activist NGOs such as Planned Parenthood of America and the International Planned Parenthood Federation. For not only had they suffered an ideological and financial defeat at Mexico City: they also seemed to understand that they had suffered a moral defeat. Many people—unenlightened, authoritarian, conservative, to be sure, but influential nonetheless—believed that the population-controllers were not only wrong but *bad*. And since a powerful conviction of the righteousness of their cause (and themselves) has been one of the chief psychological characteristics of the population-control movement for well over a century, it was this moral rejection that cut most deeply, and inflamed the controllers' determination to "go beyond Mexico City" at the next turn of the decennial conference wheel.

C-l-i-n-t-o-n Spells "Relief"?

The U.S. presidential election of November 1992 promised relief, and indeed more than relief, to those of this disposition. Bill Clinton and Al Gore had, after all, run on the most radical "social issues" platform in American history, committing themselves to federal funding of abortion-on-demand in the United States at any stage of a pregnancy while they deplored "explosive population growth" in the Third World and pledged to use federal tax dollars to fund "greater family-planning efforts" in U.S. foreign-aid programs. Moreover, the Democratic Party's most vocal activists included men and women, heterosexual and homosexual, who were deeply committed to securing in U.S. law and public policy the sexual revolution's core principle of individual autonomy and its severance of the relationship between sexual expression and marriage. Little wonder, then, that the population-controllers, determined to "go beyond Mexico City," read the electoral entrails of November 3, 1992, as a mandate for radical change in U.S. population policy and in the agenda of the forthcoming third International Conference on Population and Development.

These expectations were met in full. Indeed, among all the twists and turns of Clinton-administration policy on both the foreign and the domestic front, one constant has been a commitment to abortion-on-demand at home and massive efforts at "population control" abroad. On his first day in office, which happened to coincide with the twentieth annual "March for Life" in Washington, President Clinton signed five executive orders widening the scope of federal involvement with, and funding of, elective abortion. Rigorous pro-*Roe* litmus tests were applied to all Clinton nominees to the federal judiciary, and few doubted that the administration wished to see abortion included as a mandated "service" in any national health-care reform. Moreover, in a time of fiscal restraint, the Clintonites did not hesitate to beef up the population-control portion of their foreign-assistance budget. Thus ten months after taking office, the administration's chief foreign-aid administrator, J. Brian Atwood, announced a five-year, $75 million commitment to fund the activities of the International Planned Parenthood Federation. (Mr. Atwood defended these and other population-control expenditures on grounds that the geographically literate found bizarre, arguing as he did that the "core" of the chaos in Somalia, in which U.S. troops were then embroiled, was overpopulation. Somali vital statistics are not the world's finest, but a reasonable estimate is that Somalia, whose territory is a little larger than that of the four states California, Washington, Maryland, and Massachusetts combined, had a population in 1992 of some 7 million, which was 40 million less than the aggregate populations of those four states.[3])

Did the key players in the Clinton administration really believe that the 42.8 percent of the popular vote they garnered in 1992 constituted a genuine mandate for radical change? Or did that slim plurality impel the more ideologically fervent among them to strike while an iron likely to cool quickly was still hot? Whatever the answer, it is clear that the administration, led by Undersecretary of State for Global Affairs Timothy Wirth, decided that "going beyond Mexico City" was an insufficiently grand goal for the Cairo Conference. In league with several Scandinavian and west European countries, U.N. and World Bank population technocrats, and feminist, anti-natalist, and environmentalist NGOs, the Clintonites tried to engineer a dramatic shift in the focus at Cairo. The packaging ("Population and Development") would remain. But the content would be dramatically altered, with the earth's "carrying capacity," "gender equality, equity, and empowerment of women," and "reproductive rights" supplanting "population and development" as the issues of moment. This plan amounted to a brazen attempt to use international law and the leverage of Western foreign-aid programs to establish the sexual revolution, as lived in Stockholm and Hollywood, as *the* model of humane culture for the twenty-first century.

The Prep-Com Steamroller

This radically altered agenda first came into clear focus in April 1994, when the third meeting of the Cairo Conference preparatory committee (Prep-Com III) took place in New York. The New York Prep-Com also underscored the determination of Undersecretary Wirth and his allies not to let open debate throw sand in the gears of their political machine. Thus the chairman of Prep-Com III, as of the Cairo Conference, was Dr. Fred Sai, usually introduced as the "representative of Ghana" but in real life (so to speak) the president of the International Planned Parenthood Federation. Nongovernmental members of the U.S. delegation to the New York session included Bella Abzug, Jeannie Rosoff, president of the Alan Guttmacher Institute (the research arm of Planned Parenthood), Patricia Waak, director of the Audubon Society's population program, and staff members of the Pew Charitable Trusts and the Rockefeller Foundation, two major funders of population-control activism. American citizens who wished to challenge the regnant Clintonite orthodoxy were treated as so many irritants. A seminar sponsored by the United States Catholic Conference (USCC), a registered U.N. NGO, was denied space in the U.N. itself; the organizers of the seminar were forbidden to post notice of their meeting; and U.N. officials and population-activist NGOs contrived to schedule two other seminars at the same time as the USCC meeting. Meanwhile, the shell organization "Catholics for a Free Choice" was given room to operate within the U.N. complex.[4]

The ugliness spilled over from the NGO fringe into the Prep-Com's formal sessions. When, on April 5, Msgr. Diarmuid Martin of the Vatican delegation criticized the proposed Cairo draft document for its ethical hollowness, he was chastised publicly from the chair by Dr. Sai, who complained that the Holy See was trying to foist its notions of sexual morality on the world. Sai's remarks were boisterously applauded by a gallery packed with anti-natalist NGO activists. (Sai set something of a record in rudeness for a U.N. committee chair by the disrespect with which he treated the Holy See delegation. But his anti-Vatican bias was not substantively original: at an earlier U.N. session, Prime Minister Gro Harlem Brundtland of Norway had complained bitterly of obstacles placed in the path of the Cairo Conference by a "small state with no natural inhabitants.")

Given these dynamics, it should have come as no surprise that Prep-Com III produced a truly radical draft document for the Cairo Conference. Only 6 of its 118 pages were devoted to the conference's ostensible theme, "population and development"; the bulk of the rest of the document was given over to proposals for a lifestyle revolution of awesome proportions.

The population-controllers did rather well at Prep-Com III. No serious challenge was raised to the shibboleth of "overpopulation." Moreover, the controllers got a pledge of serious money. The draft document committed the international community to a massive increase in funding for population-control activities, from the current $6 billion to $17 billion by the year 2000. The increase was to be financed by increased American, Japanese, and Scandinavian contributions to the U.N. Population Fund (UNFPA), and by cutbacks in U.N.-sponsored education, health care, industrial development, and disaster relief.

But it was the philosophical shift embedded in the Cairo draft document that marked a sea change in the debate. For the draft document's view of the human condition and the human prospect was rooted in that concept of the "autonomous self," the radically autonomous individual, with which Americans have become all too familiar through the sexual revolution, the deconstructionist decay of the American academy, and the philosophical musings of several Supreme Court justices. "Choice," the mantra of U.S. proponents of abortion-on-demand (and "gay rights," and "alternative forms of marriage," and all the rest of it), became the antiphon of the draft Cairo document produced by Prep-Com III. And the results, to put it gently, were striking.

The Radical Moment

"Marriage" was the dog that didn't bark in the Cairo draft document. Indeed, the only time the word appeared in the document's chapter on "the family" was when Prep-Com III rightly deplored "coercion and discrimination in policies and practices related to marriage." But this absence was hardly surprising, in that the draft document, while frequently noting the importance of "the family in its various forms," said absolutely nothing about the importance of families rooted in stable marriages for the physical and mental well-being of children. Nor did the draft document have much else to say about the natural and moral bond between parents and children and its importance for achieving many of the document's laudable goals, such as improved health care and education for youngsters. Indeed, the document sundered the moral relationship between parents and teenage children by treating sexual activity as a "right" to be exercised at will, post-puberty, and by suggesting that state population and "reproductive health care" agencies be the primary interlocutors of young men and women coming to grips with their sexuality.

The Cairo draft document also proposed establishing a new category of internationally recognized human rights: "reproductive rights," with the "right" to abortion-on-demand as the centerpiece. Indeed, it seemed at times as if the codification of an internationally recognized (and, presumably, enforced) "right to abortion" was the primary goal of the Clinton administration in its Cairo policy-planning. Thus on March 16, 1994, Secretary of State Warren Christopher sent a cable to all U.S. diplomatic stations abroad, stating that "the U.S. believes that access to safe, legal, and voluntary abortion is a fundamental right of all women," and emphasizing that the U.S. objective at Cairo was to get "stronger language on the importance" of "abortion services" into the conference final report. Christopher's cable, for all its misconstrual of the state of the abortion debate in the United States, at least had the merit of intelligibility; the draft Cairo document followed the familiar U.N. pattern of Orwellian euphemism, in which coercive family-planning policies became "fertility regulation," and abortion-on-demand was transmuted into "safe motherhood" and "reproductive rights." (*U.S. News & World Report* described attempts to clarify the true meaning of this obfuscatory

New-speak as "Jesuitical deconstruction," a minor but telling example of the anti-Catholicism that permeated and fouled media coverage of the Cairo Conference.[5])

In a self-referential inconsistency familiar to U.S. veterans of the abortion wars, the Cairo draft document then married the philosophy of the imperial autonomous Self to a program of large-scale state coercion in the service of "reproductive rights," "gender equity," and, of course, population control. Parents were, again, the primary victims here, as the draft document mandated states to override parental prerogatives (known, in U.N.-speak, as "social barriers to sexual and reproductive health information and care") in the matter of adolescent sexual education. The draft document also called for state intrusion into the doctor-patient relationship: after warning that "health care providers" must not "restrict the access of adolescents to the services and information they need," the document required states to ensure that those "providers" have the proper "attitudes" toward their teenage patients. One need not doubt that the "attitudes" to be enforced here were those of Dr. Joycelyn Elders, whose career as U.S. surgeon general finally self-destructed eight months later.

The draft document produced by Prep-Com III also had a nasty totalitarian edge to it. In a striking passage that reflected the affinity between the *Kultur* of Oprah Winfrey, Phil Donahue, and Linda Bloodworth-Thomasson, on the one hand, and the agenda of Bella Abzug and International Planned Parenthood, on the other, governments were instructed to "use the entertainment media, including radio and television soap operas and drama, folk theater, and other traditional media," to proselytize for the draft document's ideology and "program of action." To insure that the usual male reprobates got the word, the draft document instructed governments to get out the message of "reproductive rights" and "gender equity" through programs that "reach men in their workplaces, at home, and where they gather for recreation," while adolescent boys should be "reached through schools, youth organizations, or wherever they congregate." In sum, there was to be no area of life—home, workplace, gym, ball park—into which state-sponsored propaganda on "reproductive rights and reproductive health" did not intrude.

Those of us who thought that this approach to public policy had been consigned to the trash heap of history in 1989 were, evidently, mistaken.

CONFRONTATION AT CAIRO

Given their success at Prep-Com III, the smug, even arrogant, self-confidence displayed by the U.N. and Clinton-administration planners of the Cairo Conference was understandable. By a highly effective manipulation of the Prep-Com's procedures, and those of the parallel NGO activities that took place in New York at the same time, the powers-that-be seemed to have perfected a *modus operandi* that would permit them to steamroller their way through the Cairo deliberations. This prospect was enhanced by the fact that more than sixty representatives of International Planned Parenthood would come to Cairo as official delegates from many nations. Not only would Cairo "go beyond Mexico City": it would adopt the radicals' lifestyle agenda without much fuss and bother. Critics, like the Holy See, could be summarily brushed aside, as they had been in New York.[6]

Yet even before the Cairo Conference convened on Labor Day 1994, some cracks were evident in the administration's coalition. It is simply assumed in the United States (and particularly in the higher altitudes of the Clinton administration) that ideological feminism, the "empowerment of women," abortion-on-demand, the libertine mores of the sexual revolution, and government propaganda (even coercion) on family planning go hand-in-glove. But that is not necessarily the way it works in other parts of the world, or even among the really radical radicals in the West. Thus, in the wake of Prep-Com III, some feminist organizations of a far more belligerent stripe than, say, the National Organization for Women began planning, for Cairo, mock trials of the World Bank, International Planned Parenthood, and the UNFPA, charging them with oppressing women through coercive governmental birth-control programs.[7] These really radical radicals would not win, in the end; but they were a harbinger of an unanticipated irony in the Cairo Conference's results.

Most tellingly, however, the conference planners did not take account of the moral power of Pope John Paul II. That Cairo did not adopt, but in fact rejected, its planners' lifestyle agenda was due to many factors: nervousness in Latin America, resistance from Islamic societies, resentment in some African countries of Western cultural imperialism. But the *sine qua non* of the defeat suffered at Cairo by the international advocates of the sexual revolution was the public campaign of opposition to the Cairo draft document mounted throughout the summer of 1994 by John Paul II.

The Pope Changes the Argument

It was not a voluble campaign. In its public (as distinguished from private, i.e., diplomatic) dimensions, it consisted of a series of twelve ten-minute reflections that the pope offered at his public audiences during June, July, and August. But by identifying the fundamental ethical errors of the draft document's approach, and by defining a compelling moral alternative to U.N.-sponsored libertinism, John Paul II set in motion a resistance movement with considerable potency. A brief review of the pope's themes will make plain the nature of the moral and cultural confrontation that eventually took place at Cairo.

■ June 12: John Paul emphasized that the right to life is *the* basic human right, "written in human nature," and the foundation of any meaningful scheme of "human rights."[8]

■ June 19: The pope talked about the family as the "primary cell" of society and as a "natural institution" with rights that any just state must respect. "Marriage," the pope taught, "as a stable union of a man and a woman who are committed to the reciprocal gift of self and open to creating new life, is not only a Christian value, but an original value of creation. The loss of this truth is not a problem for believers alone, but a danger for all humanity."[9]

■ June 22: John Paul defended the equal human dignity of women, insisted that women must not be reduced to being objects of male pleasure, and argued that "perfection for woman is not to be like man, making herself masculine to the point of losing her specific qualities as a woman; her perfection—which is also a secret of affirmation and of relative autonomy—is to be a woman, equal to man but different. In civil society and also in the Church, the equality and diversity of women must be recognized."[10]

■ June 26: The pope revisited his portrait of sexual union in marriage as a "reciprocal gift of self," noting that sexuality has a "language of its own at the service of love and cannot be lived at the purely instinctual level."[11]

■ July 3: The Holy Father reminded his listeners that unity, communion of life, and fidelity are essential to marriage, which has the character of a covenant, not merely a contract.[12]

■ July 10: John Paul argued that stable marriages were essential for the welfare of children.[13]

■ July 17: The pope taught that the Church does not support an "ideology of fertility at all costs," but rather proposes a marital ethic in which the decision "whether or not to have a child" is not "motivated by selfishness or carelessness, but by a prudent, conscious generosity that weighs the possibilities and circumstances, and especially gives priority to the welfare of the unborn child."[14]

■ July 24: The Holy Father rejected coercive or "authoritarian" family-planning programs as a violation of the married couple's basic human rights.[15]

■ July 31: John Paul taught that children are a gift to be welcomed in love, and are never to be exploited for parents' "interests or personal gratification."[16]

■ August 7: The pope argued that the foundations of justice in a state are undermined when it does not recognize the unborn child's moral claim to protection.[17]

■ August 14: The pope insisted that discrimination against women in "workplace, culture, and politics" must be eliminated in the name of an "authentic emancipation" that does not "deprive woman herself of what is primarily or exclusively hers," but rather brings the "feminine genius" into full play in public life.[18]

■ August 28: John Paul argued that radical individualism is inhuman, as is a "sexuality apart from ethical references." What Cairo should promote, the pope said, was a "culture of responsible procreation."[19]

Opening Skirmishes

Throughout the summer of 1994, Undersecretary Wirth continued to insist that "we have no fight with the Vatican."[20] But an argument of considerable amperage had, evidently, been engaged. Wirth himself began a tour of the American hierarchy, focusing on the resident U.S. cardinals; it would not be unrealistic to suggest that, in addition to explaining the administration's position, the undersecretary was searching for a weak link in the chain of American Catholic episcopal support for John Paul II and the Holy See. He did not find it. Instead, on May 29, a letter to President Clinton was hand-delivered to the White House. It was signed by the six resident U.S. cardinals—Hickey of Washington, Bernardin of Chicago, Law of Boston, O'Connor of New York, Bevilacqua of Philadelphia, and Mahony of Los Angeles —and the president of the National Conference of Catholic Bishops (NCCB), Archbishop William H. Keeler of Baltimore. The letter expressed to the President the prelates' grave concern over "your administration's promotion of abortion, contraception, sterilization, and the redefinition of the family" and urged him to reverse the administration's "destructive" agenda for Cairo.

A month later the NCCB, meeting in San Diego, unanimously adopted a statement in which the bishops, as "religious leaders and as U.S. citizens," declared themselves "outraged that our government is leading the effort to foster global acceptance of abortion."[21] And, lest it be thought that worries over Cairo were exclusively Catholic, it should be noted that a month before the cardinals' May 29 letter, eleven evangelical leaders, including Charles Colson, James Dobson, Charles Swindoll, Billy Melvin, and Bill Bright, co-signed a letter asking the administration to rescind the March 16 Christopher cable and urging the President "not to make the United States an exporter of violence and death."

By the end of the summer, the pope's decisive clarification of the moral issues at stake in Cairo had not only put the impending conference on the front pages of the prestige press but had also had a powerful political effect. Undersecretary Wirth, by now a somewhat improbable figure, continued to plead, against all the evidence, that the administration had "no fight with the Vatican." But his superiors evidently disagreed and were worried, for on August 25 Vice President Al Gore, who was to lead the U.S. delegation in the early days of the Cairo Conference, announced in a speech at the National Press Club in Washington that "the United States has not sought, does not seek, and will not seek to establish any international right to abortion." Any attempt to suggest otherwise was, he said, a "red herring."[22] Yet, as the Holy See's press spokesman, Joaquín Navarro-Valls, pointed out at a press conference in Rome on August 31, Gore's statement did not square with the draft document, whose definition of "reproductive health care" as including "pregnancy termination" had been a U.S. initiative. In what was perhaps an exercise of charity, Navarro-Valls did not make the further point that Gore's Press Club speech was also inconsistent with the Christopher cable of March 16, with the administration's domestic policy, and with its foreign-aid programs.[23]

There is some reason to believe that the Vice President was misinformed, rather than deliberately disingenuous, on these matters. And no doubt Gore was genuinely concerned about charges of administration anti-Catholicism, which had been reignited on August 19 when a Reuters story quoted Faith Mitchell, the State Department's population coordinator, as attributing Vatican disagreement with the Cairo draft document to "the fact that the conference is really calling for a new role for women, calling for girls' education and improving the status of women."[24] But whatever else it clarified or obscured, the Gore/Navarro-Valls exchange made it unmistakably clear that a great battle loomed in Cairo, where the "private sector advisers" to the U.S. delegation included Pamela Maraldo, president of Planned Parenthood of America, and (in what the administration may inexplicably have thought was a concession to religious concerns) the Rev. Joan Brown Campbell, general secretary of the National Council of Churches.

The Contest at the Conference

Perhaps the less ideologically and more politically astute among the U.S. delegates hoped that the moral issues could somehow be finessed. But on the very first day of the conference, any such hopes were dashed when Prime Minister Benazir Bhutto of Pakistan—a Harvard-educated woman who was unmistakably a major political figure—took to the rostrum to defend the "sanctity of life" on religious grounds and to condemn the Cairo draft document for trying to "impose adultery, sex education . . . and abortion" on all countries. The media, predictably, gave more attention to another woman, Norwegian prime minister Gro Harlem Brundtland, and her defense of "choice" as the essence of the moral issue of abortion. But Bhutto's impassioned rejection of abortion-on-demand, featured on page one of both the *New York Times* and the *Washington Post* and accompanied by pictures of the Pakistani and Norwegian leaders, easily won the battle of feminist iconography—and should have rebutted, once and for all, the charge that the Vatican was holding up consensus on the Cairo document for narrow sectarian reasons.[25]

The opening-day statements were followed by five days of negotiating impasse on the document's abortion language, its discussion of the family, and its approach to adolescent sexuality. During that first week, anti-Catholic sentiment and decidedly undiplomatic criticism of the Holy See were freely vented by NGO activists and official delegates alike. Nicolaas Biegman, the Dutch conference vice chairman, complained after four days that "all we read [about] is abortion, abortion, abortion. I deeply regret it. I think it's a pity."[26] Columbia's Allan Rosenfield, who represented the American College of Obstetricians and Gynecologists at Cairo, opined that "the Catholic women of the world do not buy into statements from the elderly celibate clergy."[27] Another apparent expert in ecclesiology, Alexander Sanger, president of Planned Parenthood of New York City, told the *New York Times* that "there are two churches, one where the hierarchy talks to the presidents of countries, and then there's the church of the people. The people are picking and choosing what parts of Catholicism they want to carry over to their personal lives." Colombia's Miguel Trias, who heads a government-sponsored family-planning organization, fretted that "these Latin American countries are trying to make the Vatican happy. But in 2,000 years the Vatican has never been happy."[28]

Unpleasantness was not limited to press conferences. Gail Quinn, a member of the Holy See delegation and executive director of the U.S. bishops' Pro-Life Secretariat, was booed and hissed in a formal session of the conference when she rose to explain the Vatican's objections to some abortion language in the proposed final report; the delegate from Benin had to admonish the chair, the ubiquitous Dr. Sai, that free speech was supposed to be sacrosanct in U.N. deliberations. Later, while walking past two American delegates, Quinn heard one of them say, in a stage whisper, "There goes that bitch."

It seemed that the Holy See's delegation was having a considerable impact at Cairo. As, indeed, it was. For, contrary to reports in the *Times* and elsewhere that the Holy See had suffered a significant setback, the Vatican had in fact achieved a great deal by the end of the first week of the Cairo Conference. The final report now stated, unambiguously, that "in no case should abortion be promoted as a method of family planning." The notion of enshrining abortion-on-demand as an internationally recognized basic human right—the centerpiece of the Wirth approach to Cairo—had been abandoned by its proponents, who tacitly conceded that there was no international consensus supporting the claim. The rights and responsibilities of parents with respect to their teenage children had been reaffirmed, and the worst of the euphemistic language about the structure of the family had been changed, so that the Cairo document could not be credibly appealed to on behalf of "gay marriage" and other innovations.[29]

The last major sticking point involved the "safety" of abortions, an important question for the Holy See, which believes that no abortion can be "safe" since, by definition, it results in the death of an innocent human being. The language in dispute stated that "in circumstances where abortion is legal, such abortion should be safe." At the level of moral principle, this was clearly unacceptable to the Vatican, for it was the equivalent of saying that "in circumstances where female circumcision is legal, it should be performed with Novocain." The language was finally altered to say that "in circumstances where abortion is not against the law, such abortion should be safe"—a minor change, on the surface, but one that holds out the prospect of legal reform and that does not concede the rectitude of permissive abortion laws.[30]

Reading the Box Score

The New York Times insisted on reporting these debates as a matter of "the Vatican and its few remaining allies" obstructing the course of human progress.[31] But there were other dynamics at work at Cairo, as at Bucharest and Mexico City, and it seemed possible that they could frustrate the more ambitious plans of both population-controllers and lifestyle radicals in the future. The controllers' agenda continues to cause serious concern in Latin America, Africa, and Asia, where political leaders understand that it is *their* populations, not those of Europe or North America, that are to be brought "under control."

The resistance of Islamic, Latin American, and some African countries to the lifestyle libertinism enshrined in the Cairo draft document was also of significance for the future. One need not admire the general quality of life in those societies to applaud their recognition that the sexual revolution's promises of a "permissive cornucopia" (in Zbigniew

Brzezinski's telling phrase) are a snare and a delusion.[32] And, as that recognition becomes increasingly widespread in an America struggling with unprecedented levels of illegitimacy, welfare-dependency, and spousal and child abuse, we may see a dramatic change in our domestic politics. For as the Clinton administration's defeat at Cairo graphically illustrates, you cannot have it both ways: you cannot strengthen the family and the serious moral commitments necessary to sustain the family by treating the community of father, mother, and children merely as one of a number of "lifestyle alternatives."

Over the long haul, though, the most significant development at the Cairo Conference may have been a shift in controlling paradigms: from "population control" to "the empowerment of women." As one Indonesian delegate put it toward the end of the meeting, "We have stopped calling women the receptors of contraceptives. We now call them agents of change."[33] Americans long familiar with the alliance between feminism and moral libertinism may instinctively regard this shift as simply an amplification of the moral crisis of modernity. But there were interesting suggestions at Cairo that, in other cultural contexts, the issue of "empowerment" may not cut the same way it does in western Europe and in some parts of the United States.

Benazir Bhutto's speech was one example of that intriguing possibility. For Bhutto's very presence at Cairo, coupled with what she said, posed a sharp question: Why should the "empowerment of women" be *necessarily* linked to the codification in international law (and national statutes) of the sexual revolution? American and western European pro-life feminists, the vast majority of whom are deeply committed Christians, have resolutely declined to make this connection. Perhaps the question can be pressed even further: In the developing world, why shouldn't "empowering women"—enabling them to be educated, healthy, and no longer treated as property for purposes of marriage—serve to strengthen the roles of women as wives, mothers, and primary educators of their children? Might not "the empowerment of women," in cultures whose women would regard Bella Abzug and Pamela Maraldo as something like aliens from Alpha Centauri, lead to a revitalization of the traditional family and a reaffirmation of the distinctively maternal power of women?

Joan Dunlop, president of the International Women's Health Coalition, found it "really extraordinary that in an international U.N. forum,

we are talking about sexual and reproductive health and the empowerment of women. These are things that many people of different cultures
can understand."[34] Indeed. But the question is, *how?* The travail of the
translators at Cairo suggests the volatility of this "empowerment" language (and the rest of the armamentarium of fem-speak), and the
difficulty of predicting how it might affect lives in radically different
societies and cultures. French translators had to resuscitate a nineteenth-
century term *(sante genesique)* to try to render "reproductive health" in
their language. "Family leave" had almost everybody but the Americans
stumped; the Arabic translation refers to parents' leaving each other after
a birth, while the Russian translation spoke of the entire family taking a
vacation together. The Chinese thought "sexual exploitation" was an
easy one, for they could rely on Chairman Mao's critique of capitalists
(they could also have used his doctor's memoirs, in which the chairman
is remembered as an unregenerate sexual predator who ingested ground
elks' horns as an antidote to impotence). But the Arabs were caught
between American buzz words and their own religious sensibilities.
"Sexually active unmarried individuals"—who under Islamic law are
committing criminal acts—thus became "sexually active as-yet-to-be-
married individuals." And the Russians couldn't figure out how to
translate "unwanted pregnancies" so that the phrase did not denote
"undesirable pregnancies." The Russian translation of "reproductive
health" comes out as "health that reproduces itself again and again,"
while in Arabic the phrase becomes "health concerning the begetting of
children."[35]

One veteran population activist, Jason Finkle of the University of
Michigan, worried that "all kinds of things have now been packed into
the trunk of population: women's and children's health, female literacy,
women's labor rights. I'm fearful that we've gotten away from the focus
on population size and growth."[36] Some will regard this as a development not to be feared but to be—very cautiously—celebrated.

BEYOND CAIRO

Some things that ought to have happened at Cairo didn't. There was
no concerted challenge to the shibboleth of "overpopulation," although the work of Nicholas Eberstadt, Julian Simon, Karl Zinsmeis-

ter, and others has made it clear that the term itself has no credible scientific meaning.[37] This intellectual failure, combined with the clash of moral visions at Cairo, produced a somewhat schizoid final document, which endorses voluntary measures of population control but then sets population targets whose achievement would seem to require coercive governmental intervention in family planning. The resolution of that tension will, over the next decade, tell us much about the future of population policy (and politics) at both the national and the international level.

The conference also failed to confront the U.N.'s continuing fixation on Third World development as essentially a matter of massive resource transfers from the developed to the developing world. The Holy See did heroic work at Cairo, as it had done in the months between Prep-Com III and the September conference. But it would have added even more to the debate had its representatives taken up the question of governmental criminality and its relation to the despoilment of the Third World. Materials for such a challenge were readily available in the 1987 encyclical of John Paul II, *Sollicitudo Rei Socialis,* in which the pope had urged developing nations to "reform certain unjust structures, and in particular their political institutions, in order to replace corrupt, dictatorial, and authoritarian governments with democratic and participatory ones."[38] The Holy See might also have taken a leaf from John Paul's 1991 social encyclical, *Centesimus Annus,* and boldly urged the view that human beings are *the* basic resource for development, because the source of wealth in the modern world is human creativity.[39]

At the grassroots level, it will be a while before the paradigm shift from "population control" to "empowerment of women" takes effect. Meanwhile, huge amounts of money will continue to be poured into family-planning programs, many of which are either subtly or overtly coercive. Remedial action on this front will require extreme vigilance over foreign-aid budgets; careful attention will have to be paid to the Clinton administration as it tries to square its adherence to an international agreement that flatly rejects abortion as a means of family planning with its commitment to huge increases in U.S. aid funding to organizations that actively promote precisely that evil.

So the Battle of Cairo will continue, in other venues. And it will remain, at bottom, a moral struggle: about the dignity and value of human beings, about the rights and responsibilities of women and men, about the relationship between marriage, sexuality, and the rearing of children. Thanks to John Paul II's refusal to concede the Holy See's irrelevance in accordance with the prepared media script, the moral core of the population argument was forced onto center stage at Cairo. And there it became clear, to those with eyes to see, that the mores of Hollywood, the Upper East Side, and Copenhagen were not universally admired or sought.

That, in itself, was no mean accomplishment. And it might, just might, presage a more morally and empirically serious population debate in the future.

The Meaning of the Presence of Children

Gilbert Meilaender

Why have children? The question carries its own pathos, and we might be tempted to reply that those for whom the question is a live one probably should not. But our society is greatly confused about this question. On the one hand, married couples—and sometimes unmarried individuals—go to great lengths to have "a child of their own." On the other hand, many couples have difficulty summoning the courage to proceed. They doubt their readiness—and that not only for economic reasons. Ellen Goodman wrote a column, a few years back, reflecting on a survey that had been taken to determine whether people felt "ready" to have children. She doubted the wisdom of such an undertaking.

> I know a dozen couples who can't decide to have children. They can't even decide how to decide. They want a rational actuarial kind of life-plan, and this test feeds right into their anxiety. The search is on to unearth the "right reason" to have children and to find out who are the "right people" to have them. . . . Parenting demands a risk and not a scoreboard.

Gilbert Meilaender is professor of religion at Oberlin College, Oberlin, Ohio. Among the books he has written are *The Limits of Love* (1987) and *The Theory and Practice of Virtue* (1984).

It is my aim here to explore the venture of parenthood, the inner meaning of the family bond. And because such an exploration must always have a location, I will examine the meaning of fecundity from within the perspective of Christian faith—which has, after all, been one of the principal sources of our culture's formation on this question, but which, on these questions, may help to point us in the direction of a true humanism.

Such a humanistic perspective, and something of the meaning of the presence of children, has been provocatively exemplified in P. D. James's recent novel *The Children of Men*.[1] The story is set in Great Britain in the year 2021. No children have been born anywhere in the world since 1995, a year in which all males—for reasons unknown —became infertile. We see what such a world means through the eyes of Theodore (Theo) Faron, an Oxford historian.

Because of his fascination with a woman named Julian, Theo makes contact with a revolutionary group to which she belongs. But their plans for revolution against the dictatorship ruling Britain suddenly take a back seat to an unexpected turn in the plot: Julian discovers that she is pregnant (by Luke, a priest, who is also a member of the small band of rebels). Needing help to escape detection until Julian gives birth, the group turns to Theo. He comes by night to their hiding place, unable to believe that Julian could truly be carrying a child. She places his hand on her abdomen, and he feels the child kick. Then she tells him to listen to its heartbeat. In order to do so, he kneels beside her.

> It was easier for him to kneel, so he knelt, unselfconsciously, not thinking of it as a gesture of homage but knowing that it was right that he should be on his knees. He placed his right arm around her waist and pressed his ear against her stomach. He couldn't hear the beating heart, but he could hear and feel the movements of the child, feel its life. He was swept by a tide of emotion which rose, buffeted and engulfed him in a turbulent surge of awe, excitement and terror, then receded, leaving him spent and weak.[2]

There is mystery in the presence of the newly created child—and Theo rightly kneels. But we can and should also explore a little the human meaning of this mystery.

The Venture of Parenthood

There is, I claimed at the outset, a certain pathos in the question, Why have children? It suggests a loss of spontaneous confidence in life and an impoverishment of spirit. This does not mean that such a question is unreasonable, particularly for those whose circumstances make hope difficult, though we may doubt whether they are the ones always most likely to raise the question. In any case, I do not seek to judge the difficulties facing any particular married couple or their special circumstances; rather, I seek to reflect upon the social significance of our attitude toward the presence of children.

The formation of a family is most truly human, a sign of health, when it springs from what Gabriel Marcel called "an experience of plenitude."[3] To conceive, bear, and rear a child ought to be an affirmation and a recognition: affirmation of the good of life that we ourselves were given; recognition that this life bears its own creative power to which we should be faithful. In this sense Marcel could claim that "the truest fidelity is creative."[4] The desire to have children is an expression of a deeply humanistic impulse to be faithful to the creative power of the life that is mysteriously ours. This impulse "is not essentially different from that of the artist who is the bearer of some message which he must communicate, of some flame which he must kindle and pass on. . . ."[5] The power of her art will have dried up in an artist who no longer feels impelled to create and who must ask, Why write? or, Why sing? or, Why paint? She will no longer be in touch with the powerfully creative Muses that were hers—and yet, of course, not simply hers; they were forces beyond her control in which she was a confident and hopeful participant.

This does not mean that we are most truly human when we simply reproduce often and almost by chance. We can distinguish, Marcel notes, between forming a family and producing a brood.[6] Nor does it mean that the marriage bond should be thought of simply as a means to the end of production of offspring, as if the relation of husband and wife were not itself centrally related to the meaning of our humanity. Nor yet does it mean that "planning" is inappropriate in the formation of a family, as if to be human were only to be subject to a life-force and not to exercise our freedom and reason. But granting all such provisos, there is still a sense in which planning alone cannot capture the "experience of plenitude" from which procreation, at its best, springs. There is, after all, no necessity that human beings exist —or that we ourselves *be*. That something rather than nothing exists is a mystery that lies buried in the heart of God, whose creative power and plenitude of being are the ground of our life. That life should have come into existence is in no way our doing. Within this life we can exercise a modest degree of control, but we deceive ourselves if we forget the mystery of creation that grounds our being.

To form a family cannot, therefore, be only an act of planning and control—unless we are metaphysically deceived. It must also be an act of faith and hope, what Marcel termed "the exercise of a fundamental generosity."[7] There is, as he quite rightly noted, a fundamental difference between deciding to produce an heir, or deciding to reproduce ourselves (by having a son and a daughter)—between such attitudes and a fidelity to life that is creative because a man and woman "in a sort of prodigality of their whole being, sow the seed of life without ulterior motive by radiating the life flame which has permeated them and set them aglow."[8] Years ago I read a set of newspaper articles comparing the attitude toward children of two married couples.[9] One couple had decided to have no children; the other had, at least by our contemporary standards, a large family. Certainly there was nothing illogical in the first couple's decision.

> They are distrustful as well of what children can do to a marriage. "When you have children," says Michael, "the focus changes from the couple to the kids. Suddenly everything is done for them. Well, I'm 27, I've used up a good portion of my life already. Why should I want to sacrifice for someone who's still got his whole life ahead of him?"

How instructive is the image this man uses. Life is held in a container. We must hold on to as much of it as we can, be careful not to give too much of it away, avoid pouring out the container's contents precipitously. One could not ask for a better contrast with Marcel's claim that the creation and sustaining of a family is an act of self-spending. And if there is nothing illogical about this man's attitude, there is, nonetheless, a failure to probe deeply the mystery of human life. As if our very existence were not itself an act of entirely gratuitous self-giving on the part of the Creator—an act for which no logical ground or explanation can be given! And in response to that primal act of self-giving we can respond with that fidelity to life which is itself creative—or we can turn the mystery of life into simply a problem to be controlled by our own attempts at planning and mastery.

To the extent that we moderns have understood the family as a problem to be mastered, and not a mystery to be explored faithfully, we have quite naturally come to adopt a certain attitude toward our children. They have been produced, not out of any spontaneous confidence in life, but as the result of our own planning. We are, therefore, tempted to suppose that we must—and can—become their protectors, the guarantors of their future. Paradoxically, having lost the metaphysical underpinnings of procreation as a participation in the Creator's own gracious self-spending, having lost much of the real significance of the family, we make of it more than it is. We invest it with more emotional freight than it can bear, as we cling ever more tightly to the children we have. The paradox is, in fact, understandable: to ask of an earthly good more than it can offer is an inescapable result of idolatry. In order to make of the family neither more nor less than it ought to be, we may be helped if we think of its inner meaning in two ways—as a biological community and a historical community.

The Family as Biological Community

Lines of kinship and descent embed us in the world of nature so that from birth we are individuals within a community. Like the other animals, humans "bring forth . . . according to their kinds" and, in more peculiarly human fashion, pass on to their children their image and likeness.[10] Our personhood is marked by that inheritance, for we incarnate the union of the man and the woman who are our parents. They are not simply reproducing themselves, nor are they simply a cause of which we are the effect. In reaching out to each other, they forge a community between two beings who are different and separate. When from their oneness they create a new human being, that act testifies to the truth that love for someone other than the self is a love that does not seek simply to see its own face in the loved one. This love creates community.

And the bond formed between parents and children does in fact bind; with it come obligations. Parents have, whether they want it or not, the honor and responsibility to stand before their children as God's representatives, for it is his creative power in which they are sharers. Children have that most puzzling of duties: to show gratitude for a bond in which they find themselves without in any way having chosen it. For the "problem" of their existence is simply, in miniature, the "problem" of all existence—the mystery that anything should exist at all. Hence, in what seems to be a biological fact, moral significance is embedded. The psalmist writes that children are "a heritage from the LORD."[11] The child, therefore, as a gift of God and the fruit of our fidelity to and participation in God's continuing creative work, is a sign of hope and of God's continued affirmation of the creation. Still more, the presence of the child indicates that the parents, as co-creators with God, have shared something of the mystery of divine love: their love-giving has proved to be life-giving. That such gratuitous self-spending should, in fact, give new life is the deepest mystery of God's being and is imaged faintly in the birth of a child.

We are, of course, free in many ways to transcend our embeddedness in nature, but we ought also to respect the embodied character of human life. As parents of children and children of parents, we are marked by the biological communities in which we find ourselves. We are not just free spirits, free to make of ourselves what we will. There is, in part at least, a "givenness" to our existence that limits us. Part of the task of a faithful life is to learn to receive that givenness with thanksgiving and to be trustworthy in the duties it lays upon us.

If this is in part the inner meaning of the bond of parents and children, we should be clear about one important truth. This bond may very often make us deeply happy; indeed, it may have the capacity to bring some of the greatest joys into human life. But we ought not to have children chiefly for that reason. Though the bond often fulfills us, it does not exist for the sake of our fulfillment. Parents are not reproducing themselves; they are giving birth to an-other human being, equal to them in dignity and bound to them in ties of kinship, but not created for their satisfaction. To desire a child of "one's own" is understandable, but such language should be used only with great caution. Biological parenthood does not confer possession of children. Rather, it calls us to the historical tasks of rearing, nurturing, and civilizing our children so that the next generation may achieve its relative independence. And it calls us to seek to impart that spontaneous confidence in life which is the fundamental ground of the family.

Self-giving, therefore, not self-fulfillment, lies at the heart of the parents' vocation. If such self-giving should prove to be deeply satisfying, we have reason to be thankful. But such a symmetrically satisfying result is not guaranteed, and seeking it is not the best way to prepare for the vicissitudes of parenthood. To give birth is a venture that must be carried out in hope and in faith that the Creator will continue to speak his "yes" upon the creation.

The Family as Historical Community

In love a man and a woman turn from themselves toward each other. They might, however, miss the call of creative fidelity to life and be forever content to turn toward each other alone, to turn out from themselves no more than that. But in the child, their union, as a union, quite naturally turns outward. They are not permitted to think of themselves as individuals who come together only for their own fulfillment. In the child they are given a task. Their union plays its role in a larger history, and it becomes part of their vocation to contribute to the ongoing life of a people. Certainly both Jews and Christians have commonly understood the bond of parents and children in this way.

> I will utter dark sayings from of old,
> things that we have heard and known,
> that our fathers have told us.
> We will not hide them from their children,
> but tell to the coming generation
> the glorious deeds of the LORD, and his might,
> and the wonders which he has wrought.
> He established a testimony in Jacob,
> and appointed a law in Israel,
> which he commanded our fathers
> to teach to their children;
> that the next generation might know them,
> the children yet unborn,
> and arise to tell them to their children,
> so that they should set their hope in God.[12]

In many respects this is the most fundamental task of parents: transmission of a way of life. When the son of the ancient Israelite asked, "What does this mean?," his father told again the story of the mighty acts of God, the story of their common life as a people. When a woman of Israel appeals to the biological bond and cries out to Jesus, "Blessed is the womb that bore you, and the breasts that you sucked," he responds: "Blessed rather are those who hear the word of God and keep it."[13] He points, that is, to a further bond that must be built upon the basis of biological community and is finally more crucial: initiation into a way of life. The apostle writes that fathers should not provoke their children to anger, but should "bring them up in the *paideia* and instruction of the Lord."[14] That task of *paideia,* of nurture and inculcation of a way of life, is the calling of parents.

Of course, these biblical passages refer to the transmission of a religious tradition: the story of God's care for his people. But they also point more generally to something fundamental. Parenthood is not just biological begetting. It is also history—a vocation to nurture the next generation, to initiate it into the human inheritance of knowledge and obligation. If today many feel that the family is "in crisis," or wonder why they should have children, that may be in large part because parents have little commitment to or sense of a story to pass on.

To think of the family as a biological community points us, we noted earlier, toward the importance of self-giving love. The same is true when we envision the family as a historical community. Here, even more clearly and starkly, the risk and venture of parenthood come into view. Parents commit themselves to initiating their children into the human inheritance and, more particularly, into the stories that depict their way of life. In so doing they shape, mold, and civilize their children.

But there are no guarantees that the final "product" of this process will be what the parents anticipated. Parents know this, of course, and are therefore understandably anxious about their children's future. However understandable such anxiety may be, it also constitutes a great temptation—the temptation to try to be the guarantor of our children's future, to protect them from all disappointment and suffering. To give in to such temptation would be, in effect, to deny their freedom to be an-other like us, equal to us in dignity. This means that parents must seek more than their own satisfaction in rearing their children. They must give themselves in faith and hope, recognizing that they are no more than co-creators and that they cannot shape the future.

Why Children?

Viewing the family from these two perspectives, we can understand why Marcel would suggest that parenthood, at its best, implies a certain fundamental generosity. And if this is true, if the family is a community that demands a great deal of us, we may often wonder why we should undertake the effort it involves. The ultimate answer is, I think, the one with which I began—that there is no answer if we lack all spontaneous confidence in life. But perhaps we can now press a little further and find a purpose or *telos* in the family bond. Both a social and a theological case can be made for commitment to the family, and we can begin with the lesser and move toward the greater.

Renewal of the species and rearing of the next generation might, of course, take place apart from anything remotely resembling the family. That is a very old idea. Plato had Socrates propose it when constructing the ideal city in *The Republic*. He suggests that by making kinship universal we could eliminate the divisive passions that ordinary family preference involves. In today's setting, we could establish a universal system of day-care centers to which children were given at birth and in which everyone had a hand in the care of all children —and in this way begin to approximate Socrates' proposal. If, however, the family is the sort of community I have described, doing this would make war on elements written very deeply into our nature. And no doubt Aristotle had something like that in mind when he suggested that Socrates' proposal would do more than combat divisive passion: it might also dilute a sense of concern and responsibility for those who come after us.[15]

We can expand a little upon his claim. A parent, after all, is not simply a public functionary charged with looking after a certain number of children. The special attachment that characterizes the parent-child bond serves, at its best, as a kind of guarantee of love—almost an analogue to divine grace. (That it does not always work this way indicates only that it is no more than an analogue and that quite often we are not at our best.) The child is loved unconditionally, for no particular reason. I love my children not because they are especially talented or qualified in one way or another, but simply because they have been given to me and placed in my care. And only such love, founded on no particular quality or attribute, can offer something approaching unconditional acceptance.

If I love my son because he plays the piano well, or my daughter because she executes the pick-and-roll with precision, if that is the ground of my special attachment, then it is subject to change. There can be little certainty that my commitment will endure, for it is likely that others will play both piano and basketball better. But when, by contrast, parental love is grounded in the facts of biological and historical bonding, the child lives in a setting that offers the kind of acceptance human beings need to become capable of adult commitment—a setting in which individuals who are separate but connected can grow and flourish. Thus, Michael Walzer perceptively commented that

> [o]ne might . . . liberate women from childbirth as well as parents from child care, by cloning the next generation . . . or by purchasing babies from underdeveloped countries. This is not the redistribution but the abolition of parental love, and I suspect that it would quickly produce a race of men and women incapable even of the commitment required for an affair.[16]

At least this much can be said about the social purpose of the family.

But from a Christian perspective our commitment to the family cannot and ought not to be grounded simply in its importance for our common life, for training the generation that will succeed us. However important, this remains only penultimate. The family is also something more than a basic social unit—and this something-more limits it, helping us to make of it neither more nor less than what it should be. It is a sphere in which God is at work on us, shaping and molding us, that we may become people who genuinely wish to share his life of love. The overarching interpretive rubric within which to understand the spheres of life—here, in particular, the family—is Augustine's statement that the servants of God "have no reason to regret even this life of time, for in it they are schooled for eternity."[17] The family is a school of virtue in which God sets before us, day after day, a few people whom we are to learn to love. This is the *paideia* of the heavenly Father at work upon both children and parents, building upon the love that comes naturally to us in our families, but transforming it also into the image of divine love.

Such straightforward religious talk may, of course, seem alien to the common life of our society, and no doubt it is, to some degree. Yet it may be precisely the language for which we are searching, language that points the way toward a true humanism. We tend to make of the family both too much and too little. Too much is made of it, as parents seek to reproduce themselves in their children, feverishly seek children "of their own," and try as much as possible to protect those children from all experience of suffering and sacrifice. In doing this we ask of the family more than it can give, and we place upon it expectations that must inevitably be disappointed. At the same time we make too little of the family—seldom seeing in it anything more than an arena for personal fulfillment, and failing to see it as a community that ought to transmit a way of life.

What we really need is language that can take seriously the venture of parenthood without depriving the family bond of a still greater *telos*, a larger aim and meaning. The family understood as a school of virtue —the place where citizens capable of adult commitment are formed, the place where we begin to learn the meaning of love—can provide that larger context.

The Importance of an Ideal

One might argue, of course, that the vision sketched above—whether true or false—is largely irrelevant to our circumstances. The creative fidelity to which the venture of parenthood calls us rests upon the virtue of hope—and, perhaps, many in our world have little reason to hope. Until we change the conditions and circumstances of their lives, this vision of the family is worthless. We might well be tempted to think in that way, but we would then fail to appreciate the importance of an ideal.

In his engagingly titled book *What's Wrong with the World*, G. K. Chesterton argued that his fellow citizens could not repair the defects of the family because they had no ideal at which to aim. Neither the Tory (Gudge) nor the Socialist (Hudge) viewed the family as sacred or had an image of what the family at its best might be:

The Tory says he wants to preserve family life in Cindertown; the Socialist very reasonably points out to him that in Cindertown at present there isn't any family life to preserve. But Hudge, the Socialist, in his turn, is highly vague and mysterious about whether he will try to restore it where it has disappeared. . . . The Tory sometimes talks as if he wanted to tighten the domestic bonds that do not exist; the Socialist as if he wanted to loosen the bonds that do not bind anybody. The question we all want to ask of both of them is the original ideal question, "Do you want to keep the family at all?"[18]

The result of such confusion, Chesterton thought, was that in his own day "the cultured class is shrieking to be let out of the decent home, just as the working class is shouting to be let into it."[19]

In such circumstances one needs an ideal—a point from which to begin and on the basis of which to think about the world. Chesterton began "with a little girl's hair":

> That I know is a good thing at any rate. Whatever else is evil, the pride of a good mother in the beauty of her daughter is good. It is one of those adamantine tendernesses which are the touchstones of every age and race. If other things are against it, other things must go down. . . . With the red hair of one she-urchin in the gutter I will set fire to all modern civilization. Because a girl should have long hair, she should have clean hair; because she should have clean hair, she should not have an unclean home; because she should not have an unclean home, she should have a free and leisured mother; because she should have a free mother, she should not have an usurious landlord; because there should not be an usurious land-lord, there should be a redistribution of property; because there should be a redistribution of property, there shall be a revolution. That little urchin with the gold-red hair, whom I have just watched toddling past my house, she shall not be lopped and lamed and altered; her hair shall not be cut short like a convict's; no, all the kingdoms of the earth shall be hacked about and mutilated to suit her. She is the human and sacred image; all around her the social fabric shall sway and split and fall; the pillars of society shall be shaken, and the roofs of ages come rushing down; and not one hair of her head shall be harmed.[20]

That captures vividly the importance—and the power—of an ideal. And until we rediscover the inner meaning of the venture of parent-hood as a mystery to be lived rather than a problem to be controlled, we will be ill equipped to deal with the ills we confront.

APPENDIX

Conference Participants

John Aird, senior research specialist on China, U.S. Bureau of the Census (retired).

Hadley Arkes, Edward Nye Professor of Jurisprudence, Amherst College.

E. Calvin Beisner, associate professor of interdisciplinary studies, Covenant College.

Donald Bishop, United States Information Agency.

Susan Power Bratton, assistant professor, Department of Philosophy and Religion Studies, University of North Texas.

Rodolfo A. Bulatao, senior demographer, The World Bank.

Michael Cromartie, senior fellow, Ethics and Public Policy Center.

Midge Decter, distinguished fellow, Institute on Religion and Public Life.

Nicholas Eberstadt, visiting scholar, American Enterprise Institute, and visiting fellow, Harvard Center for Population and Development Studies.

Note: Participants are identified with their positions at the time of the conference (October 1993), not at the time of publication.

Robert Engelman, director of population and environment, Population Action International.

Jean Guilfoyle, director, Population Research Institute.

Steve Hayward, research and editorial director, Pacific Research Institute.

Jacqueline Kasun, professor of economics, Humboldt State University.

Jo Kwong, director of public affairs and environmental research associate, Atlas Economic Research Foundation.

Diarmuid Martin, undersecretary, Pontifical Council for Justice and Peace.

James McHugh, Roman Catholic Bishop of Camden, New Jersey.

Gilbert Meilaender, professor of religion, Oberlin College.

Sheldon Richman, senior editor, The Cato Institute.

Robert Royal, vice-president, Ethics and Public Policy Center.

Herbert Schlossberg, senior research scholar, The Fieldstead Institute.

Julian Simon, professor of business and economics, University of Maryland.

Tim Stafford, senior writer, *Christianity Today*.

Margaret O'Brien Steinfels, editor, *Commonweal*.

Paul Thompson, vice-president for advocacy and education, World Vision International.

George Weigel, president, Ethics and Public Policy Center.

Karl Zinsmeister, editor, *The American Enterprise*.

Notes

CHAPTER 1
Midge Decter

1. Paul and Anne Ehrlich, *The Population Explosion* (New York: Simon and Schuster, 1990).

2. Norman Thomas, "A Socialist's Viewpoint," *Birth Control Review,* September 1929, cited in Ellen Chesler, *Women of Valor* (New York: Simon and Schuster, 1992), 215.

3. Christopher Tietze, "Fertility Control," *International Encyclopedia of the Social Sciences* (Crowell, Collier, and MacMillan, 1968), 5:388.

4. Shulamith Firestone, *The Dialectic of Sex* (New York: Bantam Books, 1971).

5. Garrett Hardin, "The Tragedy of the Commons," *Science,* December 13, 1968.

6. Ehrlich, *The Population Explosion*.

7. Serious astronomers maintain that the so-called depletion of the ozone layer has nothing to do with "gases" and is not in fact "depletion" but rather the tracing of a natural cycle from its peak to its lowest point; as for acid rain, the verdict is still far from in on what causes it, what its actual effects are, and what is responsible for its recent decrease (see *New York Times,* September 12, 1993).

8. Ehrlich, *The Population Explosion*.

9. Garrett Hardin, *Exploring New Ethics for Survival: The Voyage of the Spaceship Beagle* (New York: Viking, 1972),

CHAPTER 2
Nicholas Eberstadt

1. T. J. Samuel, "The Development of India's Policy of Population Control," *Milbank Memorial Fund Quarterly* 44(1966):1, 54.

2. United Nations, *Review of Recent National Demographic Target-Setting* (New York: U.N. Department of International Economic and Social Affairs, 1989), 11-14, 26-28.

3. United Nations, *World Population Monitoring 1989* (New York: U.N. Department of International Economic and Social Affairs, 1989), 55.

4. United Nations, *World Population Prospects, The 1992 Revision* (New York: United Nations, 1993), table A-13. Projections cited are total fertility rates for the 1990-95 period.

5. Paul Lewis, "Curb on Population Growth Needed Urgently, U.N. Says," *New York Times,* April 30, 1992, A12.

6. Paul R. Ehrlich, *The Population Bomb* (New York: Ballantine Books, 1968).

7. Donnella H. Meadows et al., *Limits to Growth: A Report for the Club of Rome's Project on the Predicament of Mankind* (New York: Universe Books, 1972).

8. Nathan Keyfitz, "The Limits of Population Forecasting," *Population and Development Review* 7(1981):4.

9. William Petersen, *Population* (New York: Macmillan, 1975), chap. 9.

10. World Bank, *World Development Report 1993* (New York: Oxford University Press), 238, 290.

11. Charles Tilly, "Introduction," in Charles Tilly and Lutz K. Berkner, eds., *Historical Studies of Changing Fertility* (Princeton: Princeton University Press, 1975), 3.

12. World Bank, *World Development Report 1985,* 174, 212.

13. Derived from United Nations, *Demographic Yearbook 1991* (New York: United Nations., 1993), 19-21.

14. Irving B. Kravis et al., *International Comparisons of Real Product and Purchasing Power* (Baltimore: Johns Hopkins University Press, 1978).

15. World Bank, *World Development Report 1993,* chap. 2.

16. Dan Usher, *The Measurement of Economic Growth* (New York: Columbia University Press, 1980), 246.

17. United Nations, *Demographic Yearbook 1991,* table 3.

18. United Nations, *World Population Prospects: The 1992 Revision,* table A-17.

19. World Bank, *World Development Report 1993,* 290-91.

20. For a definitive critique of the "unmet need" argument, see Charles F. Westoff, "Is the 'KAP Gap' Real?," *Population and Development Review* 14(1988):2.

21. Theodore W. Schultz, "The Value of the Ability to Deal with Disequilibria," *Journal of Economic Literature* 13(1975):3.

22. P. T. Bauer, "The Population Explosion: Myths and Realities," in *Equality, The Third World, and Economic Delusion* (Cambridge: Harvard University Press, 1981).

23. Albert O. Hirschmann, *Development Projects Observed* (Washington, D.C.: Brookings Institution, 1967).

24. David Morowetz, *Twenty-five Years of Economic Development, 1950-1975* (Washington, D.C.: World Bank, 1977), 22.

Robert Engelman

1. "Population Perspective Is Widening: Interview with Louise Lassonde (of United Nations Population Fund)," *People & the Planet* 1, no. 1 (1992): 12-13.

2. For a provocative speculation on the role of population size and growth in problems apart from economic and environmental, see Charles C. Mann, "How Many Is Too Many?," *The Atlantic,* February 1993, 47-67.

3. Nicholas D. Kristof, "A U.N. Agency May Leave China Over Coercive Population Control," *New York Times,* May 15, 1993, A1.

4. Ronald Freedman, "Family Planning Programs in the Third World," *Annals of the American Academy for Political and Social Science* 510 (July 1990): 33-43.

5. John Bongaarts, W. Parker Mauldin, and James F. Phillips, "The Demographic Impact of Family Planning Programs," *Studies in Family Planning,* vol. 21, no. 6.

6. Personal communication with Steven W. Sinding of the Rockefeller Foundation.

7. Steven W. Sinding, "Getting to Replacement: Bridging the Gap between Individual Rights and Demographic Goals," paper delivered at International Planned Parenthood Federation Family Planning Congress, October 23-25, 1992, Delhi, India.

CHAPTER 4

Amartya Sen

1. This paper draws on my lecture arranged by the "Eminent Citizens Committee for Cairo '94" at the United Nations in New York on April 18, 1994, and also on research supported by the National Science Foundation.

2. Paul Ehrlich, *The Population Bomb* (Ballantine, 1968). More recently Paul Ehrlich and Anne H. Ehrlich have written *The Population Explosion* (Simon and Schuster, 1990).

3. Garrett Hardin, *Living Within Limits* (Oxford University Press, 1993).

4. Thomas Robert Malthus, *Essay on the Principle of Population As It Affects the Future Improvement of Society with Remarks on the Speculation of Mr. Godwin, M. Condorcet, and Other Writers* (London: J. Johnson, 1798), chap. 8; in the Penguin Classics edition (1982), *An Essay on the Principle of Population,* 123.

5. See Simon Kuznets, *Modern Economic Growth* (Yale University Press, 1966).

6. Note by the Secretary-General of the United Nations to the Preparatory Committee for the International Conference on Population and Development, Third Session, A/Conf.171/PC/5, February 18, 1994, 30.

7. Philip Morris Hauser's estimates are presented in the National Academy of Sciences publication *Rapid Population Growth: Consequences and Policy Implications,* vol. 1 (Johns Hopkins University Press, 1971). See also Simon Kuznets, *Modern Economic Growth,* chap. 2.

8. For an important collection of papers on these and related issues see Sir Francis Graham-Smith, F.R.S., editor, *Population — The Complex Reality: A Report of the Population Summit of the World's Scientific Academies,* issued by the Royal Society and published in the United States by North American Press, Golden, Colorado. See also D. Gale Johnson and Ronald D. Lee, editors, *Population Growth and Economic Development: Issues and Evidence* (University of Wisconsin Press, 1987).

9. Garrett Hardin, *Living Within Limits,* 274.

10. Paul Kennedy, who has discussed important problems in the distinctly "social" aspects of population growth, has pointed out that this debate "has, in one form or another, been with us since then," and "it is even more pertinent today than when

Malthus composed his *Essay*," in *Preparing for the Twenty-first Century* (Random House, 1993), 5-6.

11. On the importance of "enlightenment" traditions in Condorcet's thinking, see Emma Rothschild, "Condorcet and the Conflict of Values," forthcoming in *The Historical Journal*.

12. Marie Jean Antoine Nicholas de Caritat Marquis de Condorcet's *Esquisse d'un Tableau Historique des Progrès de l'Esprit Humain, Xe Epoque* (1795). English translation by June Barraclough, *Sketch for a Historical Picture of the Progress of the Human Mind*, with an introduction by Stuart Hampshire (Weidenfeld and Nicolson, 1955), 187-92.

13. T. R. Malthus, *A Summary View of the Principle of Population* (London: John Murray, 1830); in the Penguin Classics edition (1982), 243; italics added.

14. On practical policies, including criticism of poverty relief and charitable hospitals, advocated for Britain by Malthus and his followers, see William St. Clair, *The Godwins and the Shelleys: A Biography of a Family* (Norton, 1989).

15. Malthus, *Essay on the Principle of Population*, chap. 17; in the Penguin Classics edition (1982), *An Essay on the Principle of Population*, 198-99. Malthus showed some signs of weakening in this belief as he grew older.

16. Gerard Piel, *Only One World: Our Own to Make and to Keep* (Freeman, 1992).

17. For discussions of these empirical connections, see R. A. Easterlin, editor, *Population and Economic Change in Developing Countries* (University of Chicago Press, 1980); T. P. Schultz, *Economics of Population* (Addison Wesley, 1981); J. C. Caldwell, *Theory of Fertility Decline* (Academic Press, 1982); E. King and M. A. Hill, editors, *Women's Education in Developing Countries* (Johns Hopkins University Press, 1992); Nancy Birdsall, "Economic Approaches to Population Growth" in *The Handbook of Development Economics*, edited by H. B. Chenery and T. N. Srinivasan (Amsterdam: North Holland, 1988); Robert Cassen et al., *Population and Development: Old Debates, New Conclusions* (New Brunswick: Overseas Development Council/Transaction Publishers, 1994).

18. World Bank, *World Development Report 1994* (Oxford University Press, 1994), Table 25, 210-11.

19. Ibid., Table 2.

20. These issues are discussed in my joint book with Jean Drèze, *Hunger and Public Action* (Oxford University Press, 1989), and three volumes edited by us, *The Political Economy of Hunger* (Oxford University Press, 1990), and also in my paper "Economic Regress: Concepts and Features," *Proceedings of the World Bank Annual Conference on Development Economics 1993* (World Bank, 1994).

21. This is confirmed by, among other statistics, the food production figures regularly presented by the United Nations Food and Agricultural Organization (see the *FAO Quarterly Bulletin of Statistics*, and also the *FAO Monthly Bulletins*).

22. For a more detailed picture and references to data sources, see my "Population and Reasoned Agency: Food, Fertility and Economic Development," in *Population, Economic Development, and the Environment*, edited by Kerstin Lindahl-Kiessling and Hans Landberg (Oxford University Press, 1994); see also the other contributions in this volume. The data presented here have been slightly updated from later publications of the FAO.

23. On this see my *Poverty and Famines* (Oxford University Press, 1981).

24. See UNCTAD VIII, Analytical Report by the UNCTAD Secretariat to the

Conference (United Nations, 1992), Table V-S, 235. The period covered is between 1979-81 and 1988-90. These figures and related ones are discussed in greater detail in my paper "Population and Reasoned Agency," cited in note 22.

25. World Bank, *Price Prospects for Major Primary Commodities,* vol. 2 (World Bank, March 1993), Annex Tables 6, 12, and 18.

26. Condorcet, *Esquisse d'un Tableau Historique;* in the 1968 reprint, 187.

27. The importance of "local" environmental issues is stressed and particularly explored by Partha Dasgupta in *An Inquiry into Well-Being and Destitution* (Oxford University Press, 1993).

28. In a forthcoming monograph by Jean Drèze and myself tentatively called "India: Economic Development and Social Opportunities," we discuss the importance of women's political agency in rectifying some of the more serious lapses in Indian economic and social performance—not just pertaining to the deprivation of women themselves.

29. See Jean Drèze and Amartya Sen, *Hunger and Public Action* (Oxford University Press, 1989), which also investigates the remarkable success of some poor countries in providing widespread educational and health services.

30. World Bank, *World Development Report 1994,* 212; and *Sample Registration System: Fertility and Mortality Indicators 1991* (New Delhi: Ministry of Home Affairs, 1993).

31. See the discussions, and the literature cited, in Gita Sen, Adrienne German, and Lincoln Chen, editors, *Population Policies Reconsidered: Health, Empowerment, and Rights* (Harvard Center for Population and Development Studies/International Women's Health Coalition, 1994).

32. On the actual processes involved, see T. N. Krishnan, "Demographic Transition in Kerala: Facts and Factors," in *Economic and Political Weekly,* vol. 11 (1976), and P. N. Mari Bhat and S. I. Rajan, "Demographic Transition in Kerala Revisited," in *Economic and Political Weekly,* vol. 25 (1990).

33. See, for example, Robin Jeffrey, "Culture and Governments: How Women Made Kerala Literate," in *Pacific Affairs,* vol. 60 (1987).

34. On this see Amartya Sen, "More Than 100 Million Women Are Missing," *New York Review of Books,* December 20, 1990; Ansley J. Coale, "Excess Female Mortality and the Balance of the Sexes: An Estimate of the Number of 'Missing Females,'" *Population and Development Review,* no. 17 (1991); Amartya Sen, "Missing Women," *British Medical Journal,* no. 304 (March 1992); Stephan Klasen, "Missing Women Reconsidered," *World Development,* forthcoming.

35. Tamil Nadu has benefited from an active and efficient voluntary program of family planning, but these efforts have been helped by favorable social conditions as well, such as a high literacy rate (the second highest among the sixteen major states), a high rate of female participation in work outside the home (the third highest), a relatively low infant-mortality rate (the third lowest), and a traditionally higher age of marriage. See also T. V. Antony, "The Family Planning Programme—Lessons from Tamil Nadu's Experience," *Indian Journal of Social Science,* vol. 5 (1992).

36. World Bank and Population Reference Bureau, *Success in a Challenging Environment: Fertility Decline in Bangladesh* (World Bank, 1993).

CHAPTER 5

George Weigel

1. Cf. my study, *The Final Revolution: The Resistance Church and the Collapse of Communism* (New York: Oxford University Press, 1992), 26-30.

2. Cf. Stephen Mosher, *A Mother's Ordeal: One Woman's Fight Against China's One-Child Policy* (New York: Harcourt, Brace, 1993).

3. John M. Goshko, "Planned Parenthood Gets AID Grant," *Washington Post,* November 23, 1993, A12-13.

4. See Dennis Poust, "Hostile U.N. Prep Session," *Catholic New York,* April 21, 1994. The mainstream press seemed wholly uninterested in these strong-arm tactics, which were, however, widely reported in pro-life newsletters and magazines.

5. Emily MacFarquhar, "Population Wars," *U.S. News & World Report,* September 12, 1994, 55.

6. Or, indeed, as they had been before the New York meeting. On March 18, 1994, Pope John Paul II met at the Vatican with Mrs. Nafis Sadik, secretary general of the UNFPA. The pope expressed his concern that the draft document to be debated at Prep-Com III tended "to promote an internationally recognized right to abortion on demand without any restriction, in a manner which goes beyond what even now is unfortunately accepted by the laws of some nations." The pope also told Mrs. Sadik that "what the Church calls responsible parenthood is not a question of unlimited procreation," nor was it based on a "lack of awareness of what is involved in raising children." Rather, the Church sought "the empowerment of couples to use their inviolable liberty wisely and responsibly, taking into account social and demographic realities as well as moral criteria." These concerns were dismissed (sometimes rudely, as we saw earlier), when they were not simply ignored, at Prep-Com III. For the full text of the pope's remarks to Mrs. Sadik, see *Origins* 23, no. 31 (March 31, 1994): 716-19.

7. MacFarquhar, "Population Wars," 56.

8. *L'Osservatore Romano,* English weekly edition, June 15, 1994, 1-2.

9. Ibid., June 22, 1994, 1.

10. Ibid., June 29, 1994, 11.

11. Ibid., 1-2.

12. Ibid., July 6, 1994, 1.

13. Ibid., July 13, 1994, 1.

14. Ibid., July 20, 1994, 1.

15. Ibid., July 27, 1994, 1-2.

16. Ibid., August 3, 1994, 1.

17. Ibid., August 10-17, 1994, 2.

18. Ibid., August 24, 1994, 2.

19. Ibid., August 31, 1994, 1.

20. See David Von Drehle, "Population Summit Has Pope Worried," *Washington Post,* June 16, 1994, A30.

21. See *Origins* 24, no. 9 (July 21, 1994): 170-71, for the full text of the bishops' statement.

22. "Remarks Prepared for Delivery by Vice President Al Gore, National Press

Club, Washington, D.C., Thursday, August 25, 1994" (Washington: Office of the Vice President), 8.

23. See Christine Gorman, "Clash of Wills in Cairo," *Time,* September 12, 1994, 56. For the full text of Navarro-Valls's statement, see *Origins* 24, no. 14 (September 15, 1994): 247-48.

24. This charge of misogyny against an institution that has done more than any other in the world to foster the education of women was rebutted in a half-page "Open Letter to the President" in the August 29 *New York Times;* the letter was signed by the heads of major Catholic women's organizations and several prominent female Catholic intellectuals.

In the same Reuters report in which Ms. Mitchell suggested that the Church wanted to deny women an education, State Department spokesman Mike McCurry warned the Vatican against negotiating with Iran. A week later, in Cairo, American delegates were seen openly negotiating compromise language on abortion and "reproductive rights" with Iranian delegates. (See Deborah Zabarenko, "U.S. Works to 'Lower Volume' on Population Debate," Reuters World Service, August 19, 1994.)

25. See Boyce Rensberger, "Explosive Abortion Issue Refueled at Forum," *Washington Post,* September 6, 1994, 1, 13, and Barbara Crossette, "Population Meeting Opens With Challenge to the Right," *New York Times,* September 6, 1994, A1, A9. Throughout the Cairo Conference, the *Times,* as is its wont, gave extensive "soundbite" space to such radical dissident Catholics as Frances Kissling and Daniel Maguire, neither of whom has any discernible constituency or intellectual standing in mainstream American Catholicism.

26. Alan Cowell, "As Abortion Fight Rages, Population-Plan Accord Nears," *New York Times,* September 9, 1994, A10.

27. Barbara Crossette, "Vatican Drops Fight Against U.N. Population Document," *New York Times,* September 10, 1994, A5. The headline suggests precisely how detached the *Times*'s coverage was from the cultural and political realities of the Cairo Conference.

28. Barbara Crossette, "Vatican Holds Up Abortion Debate at Talks in Cairo," *New York Times,* September 8, 1994, A8.

29. A month after the Cairo Conference, Undersecretary Wirth told an audience at the Johns Hopkins University's Nitze School of Advanced International Studies that "the Cairo conference was a very clear and resounding win for the United States of America," a.k.a. the Clinton administration. Applying to the undersecretary's statement one of the iron laws of Washington "spin control"—i.e., that when you have to keep announcing that you've won, you've really lost—we may draw the appropriate conclusions about the Wirthian hermeneutic on Cairo. (See Mark Zimmerman, "Cairo Conundrum," *Catholic Standard* [Washington, D.C.], October 13, 1994, 1, 3.)

30. The Holy See's last formal statement at Cairo identified those parts of the final document with which it agreed and those parts it still found objectionable. Arguing that the Holy See's views were shared by "many, believers and nonbelievers alike, in every country, of the world," Archbishop Renato Martino, the head of the Vatican delegation, welcomed the document's "affirmations against all forms of coercion in population policies," its recognition of the family as "the basic unit of society," and its stress on "women's advancement and the improvement of women's status through

education and better health care services." The archbishop then deplored the fact that the final document "recognizes abortion as a dimension of population policy and indeed of primary health care, even though it does stress that abortion should not be promoted as a means of family planning and urges nations to find alternatives to abortion. The preamble implies that the document does not contain the affirmation of a new internationally recognized right to abortion." (The full text of Archbishop Martino's statement, including the text of the Holy See's "annexed note" to the final document, may be found in *Origins* 24, no. 15 (September 22, 1994): 257-60.

31. Cowell, "As Abortion Fight Rages."

32. See Zbigniew Brzezinski, *Out of Control: Global Turmoil on the Eve of the Twenty-First Century* (New York: Charles Scribner's Sons, 1993), especially 64-74.

33. Cited in Crossette, "Vatican Drops Fight."

34. Peter Waldman, "Lost in Translation," *Wall Street Journal,* September 13, 1994, 1.

35. All citations, ibid.

36. Ibid.

37. See Nicholas Eberstadt, "What You Won't Hear at Cairo," *Wall Street Journal,* September 6, 1994; Julian Simon, "The Population Distraction," *New York Times,* August 21, 1994; and George Weigel, "It's Voodoo Science," *Los Angeles Times,* September 5, 1994.

38. *Sollicitudo Rei Socialis,* 44.

39. On this point, see William McGurn, "The Population Problem," *National Review,* September 12, 1994, 64-68.

AFTERWORD

Gilbert Meilaender

1. P. D. James, *The Children of Men* (New York: Knopf, 1993).

2. Ibid., 153f.

3. Gabriel Marcel, "The Mystery of the Family," in *Homo Viator: Introduction to a Metaphysic of Hope* (New York: Harper Torchbooks, 1962), 88.

4. Ibid., 90.

5. Ibid., 88.

6. Ibid., 87. There is, of course, also a difference between a *brood* and a *large family.* And for those who take seriously the idea that the truest fidelity is to be creative— the idea that our own creativity participates in and mirrors the divine creative power —there is something to be said, at least in principle, for the large family. Marcel himself makes the point nicely in another essay, "The Creative Vow as the Essence of Fatherhood," also collected in *Homo Viator:*

> [I]t would be impossible to exaggerate the extent of the difference which separates a large family from a family of one or two children: a difference comparable to that which in the philosophy of Bergson separates the Enclosed from the Open. It is a difference of atmosphere in the first place: that which exists between fresh air and the air in a confined space. We must, however, go much further. By the

multiplicity, the unpredictable variety of the relationships which it embraces, the large family really presents the character of a creation . . . [113].

7. Ibid., 91.

8. Ibid., 88.

9. *Washington Post,* August 7, 1975.

10. Genesis 1:24; 5:3.

11. Psalm 127:3.

12. Psalm 78:2-7.

13. Luke 11:27-28.

14. Ephesians 6:4.

15. Aristotle, *Politics,* II:iii, 1261*b*. Cf. A. W. Price, *Love and Friendship in Plato and Aristotle* (Oxford: Clarendon Press, 1989), 188.

16. Michael Walzer, *Spheres of Justice* (New York: Basic Books, 1983), 238f.

17. Augustine, *City of God,* I, 29.

18. G. K. Chesterton, *What's Wrong with the World,* vol. 4 of *Collected Works* (San Francisco: Ignatius Press, 1987), 212.

19. Ibid., 65.

20. Ibid., 217f.

Index of Names